THE

ANTI-SLAVERY CRUSADE

IN AMERICA

I AM I NOT A MAN AND A BROTHER?

CORRESPONDENCE BETWEEN THE
HON. F. H. ELMORE
AND
JAMES G. BIRNEY

ARNO PRESS
&
THE NEW YORK TIMES
NEW YORK   1969

CORRESPONDENCE BETWEEN THE
HON. F. H. ELMORE AND JAMES G. BIRNEY

No. 8.

THE

ANTI-SLAVERY EXAMINER.

CORRESPONDENCE,

BETWEEN THE

Hon. F. H. ELMORE,

ONE OF THE SOUTH CAROLINA DELEGATION IN CONGRESS,

AND

JAMES G. BIRNEY,

ONE OF THE SECRETARIES OF THE AMERICAN ANTI-SLAVERY SOCIETY.

NEW-YORK:

PUBLISHED BY THE AMERICAN ANTI-SLAVERY SOCIETY,
No. 143 NASSAU STREET.
1838.

This periodical contains 5 sheets.—Postage under 100 miles, 7 1-2 cts. ; over 100 miles, 12 1-2 cts.

☞ *Please read and circulate.* ☜

REMARKS IN EXPLANATION.

Anti-Slavery Office, *New York, May* 24, 1838.

In January, a tract entitled "Why work for the slave?" was issued from this office by the agent for the *Cent-a-week Societies.* A copy of it was transmitted to the Hon. John C. Calhoun ;—to *him,* because he has seemed, from the first, more solicitous than the generality of Southern politicians, to possess himself of accurate information about the Anti-Slavery movement. A note written by me accompanied the tract, informing Mr. Calhoun, why it was sent to him.

Not long afterward, the following letter was received from the Hon. F. H. Elmore, of the House of Representatives in Congress. From this and another of his letters just now received, it seems, that the Slaveholding Representatives in Congress, after conferring together, appointed a committee, of their own number, to obtain authentic information of the intentions and progress of the Anti-Slavery associations,—and that Mr. Elmore was selected, as the *South Carolina* member of the Committee.

Several other communications have passed between Mr. Elmore and me. They relate, chiefly, however, to the transmission and reception of Anti-slavery publications, which he requested to be sent to him,—and to other matters not having any connection with the merits of the main subject. It is, therefore, thought unnecessary to publish them. It may be sufficient to remark of all the communications received from Mr. Elmore—that they are characterized by exemplary courtesy and good temper, and that they bear the impress of an educated, refined, and liberal mind.

It is intended to circulate this correspondence throughout the *whole country*. If the information it communicates be important for southern Representatives in Congress, it is not less so for their Constituents. The Anti-slavery movement has become so important in a National point of view, that no statesman can innocently remain ignorant of its progress and tendencies. The facts stated in my answer may be relied on, in proportion to the degree of accuracy to which they lay claim; —the arguments will, of course, be estimated according to their worth

JAMES G. BIRNEY.

CORRESPONDENCE.

WASHINGTON CITY, FEB. 16, 1838

To Jas. G. Birney, Esq., *Cor. Sec. A. A. S. Soc.*

Sir:—A letter from you to the Hon. John C. Calhoun, dated 29th January last, has been given to me, by him, in which you say, (in reference to the abolitionists or Anti- Slavery Societies,) " we have nothing to conceal—and should you desire any information as to our procedure, it will be cheerfully communicated on [my] being apprised of your wishes." The frankness of this unsolicited offer indicates a fairness and honesty of purpose, which has caused the present communication, and which demands the same full and frank disclosure of the views with which the subjoined inquiries are proposed.

Your letter was handed to me, in consequence of a duty assigned me by my delegation, and which requires m. to procure all the authentic information I can, as to the nature and intentions of yours and similar associations, in order that we may, if we deem it advisable, lay the information before our people, so that they may be prepared to decide understandingly, as to the course it becomes them to pursue on this all important question. If you "have nothing to conceal," and it is not imposing too much on, what may have been, an unguarded proffer, I will esteem your compliance as a courtesy to an opponent, and be pleased to have an opportunity to make a suitable return. And if, on the other hand, you have the least difficulty or objection, I trust you will not hesitate to withhold the information sought for, as I would not have it, unless as freely given, as it will, if deemed expedient, be freely used.

I am, Sir,

Your ob'd't serv't,

F. H. ELMORE, of S. C.

QUESTIONS for J. G. Birney, Esq., Cor. Sec. A. A. S. Society.

1. How many societies, affiliated with that of which you are the Corresponding Secretary, are there in the United States ? And how many members belong to them *in the aggregate?*

2. Are there any other societies similar to yours, and not affiliated with it, in the United States ? and how many, and what is the aggregate of their members ?

3. Have you affiliation, intercourse or connection with any similar societies out of the United States, and in what countries ?

4. Do your or similar societies exist in the Colleges and other Literary institutions of the non-slaveholding States, and to what extent ?

5. What do you estimate the numbers of those who co-operate in this matter at ? What proportion do they bear in the population of the Northern states, and what in the Middle non-slaveholding states ? Are they increasing, and at what rate ?

6, What is the object your associations aim at ? does it extend to the abolition of slavery only in the District of Columbia, or in the whole slave country ?

7. By what means, and under what power, do you propose to carry your views into effect ?

8. What has been for three years past, the annual income of your societies ? and how is it raised ?

9. In what way, and to what purposes, do you apply these funds ?

10. How many printing presses and periodical publications have you ?

11. To what classes of persons do you address your publications, and are they addressed to the judgment, the imagination, or the feelings ?

12. Do you propagate your doctrines by any other means than oral and written discussions,—for instance, by prints and pictures in manufactures—say pocket handkerchiefs, &c. Pray, state the various modes ?

13. Are your hopes and expectations increased or lessened by the events of the last year, and, especially, by the action of this Congress ? And will your exertions be relaxed or increased ?

14. Have you any permanent fund, and how much ?

ANTI-SLAVERY OFFICE, *New York, March* 8, **1838**

Hon. F. H. ELMORE,

Member of Congress from S. Carolina:

SIR,—I take pleasure in furnishing the information you have so politely asked for, in your letter of the 16th ult., in relation to the Amer
ican Anti-Slavery Society;—and trust, that this correspondence, by presenting in a sober light, the objects and measures of the society, may contribute to dispel, not only from your own mind, but—if it be diffused throughout the South—from the minds of our fellow-citizens there generally, a great deal of undeserved prejudice and groundless alarm. I cannot hesitate to believe, that such as enter on the examination of its claims to public favour, without bias, will find that it aims intelligently, not only at the promotion of the interests of the slave, but of the master, —not only at the re-animation of the Republican principles of our Constitution, but at the establishment of the Union on an enduring basis.

I shall proceed to state the several questions submitted in your letter, and answer them, in the order in which they are proposed. You ask,—

" 1. *How many societies, affiliated with that of which you are corresponding secretary, are there in the United States?   And how many members belong to them* IN THE AGGREGATE ?"

ANSWER.—Our anniversary is held on the Tuesday immediately preceding the second Thursday in May. Returns of societies are made only a short time before. In May, 1835, there were 225 auxiliaries reported. In May, 1836, 527. In May, 1837, 1006. Returns for the anniversary in May next have not come in yet. It may, however, be safely said, that the increase, since last May, is not less than 400.* Of late, the multiplication of societies has not kept pace with the progress of our principles. Where these are well received, our agents are not so careful to organize societies as in former times, when our numbers were few ; *societies, now,* being not deemed so necessary for the advancement of our cause   The auxiliaries average not less than 80 members each ; making an aggregate of 112,480. Others estimate the auxiliaries at 1500, and the average of members at 100. I give you, what I believe to be the lowest numbers.

" 2. *Are there any other societies similar to yours, and not affiliated with it in the United States?   And how many, and what is the aggregate of their members ?*"

---

* The number reported for May was three hundred and forty, making, in the aggregate, 1346.—*Report for May*, 1838.

ANSWER.—Several societies have been formed in the Methodist connection within the last two years,—although most of the Methodists who are abolitionists, are members of societies auxiliary to the American. These societies have been originated by Ministers, and others of weight and influence, who think that their brethren can be more easily persuaded, as a religious body, to aid in the anti-slavery movement by this twofold action. None of the large religious denominations bid fairer soon to be on the side of emancipation than the Methodist. Of the number of the Methodist societies that are not auxiliary, I am not informed.—The ILLINOIS SOCIETY comes under the same class. The REV. ELIJAH P. LOVEJOY, the corresponding secretary, was slain by a mob, a few days after its organization. It has not held a meeting since; and I have no data for stating the number of its members. It is supposed not to be large.—Neither is the DELAWARE SOCIETY, organized, a few weeks ago, at Wilmington, auxiliary to the American. I have no information as to its numbers.—The MANUMISSION SOCIETY in this city, formed in 1785, with JOHN JAY its first, and ALEXANDER HAMILTON its second president, might, from its name, be supposed to be affiliated with the American. Originally, its object, so far as regarded the slaves, and those illegally held in bondage *in this state*, was, in a great measure, similar. Slavery being extinguished in New-York in 1827, as a state system, the efforts of the Manumission Society are limited now to the rescue, from kidnappers and others, of such persons as are really free by the laws, but who have been reduced to slavery. Of the old Abolition societies, organized in the time, and under the influence of Franklin and Rush and Jay, and the most active of their coadjutors, but few remain. Their declension may be ascribed to this defect,—they did not inflexibly ask for *immediate* emancipation.—The PENNSYLVANIA ABOLITION SOCIETY, formed in 1789, with DR. FRANKLIN, president, and DR. RUSH, secretary, is still in existence—but unconnected with the American Society. Some of the most active and benevolent members of both the associations last named, are members of the American Society. Besides the societies already mentioned, there may be in the country a few others of anti-slavery name; but they are of small note and efficiency, and are unconnected with this.

"3. *Have you affiliation, intercourse, or connection with any similar societies out of the United States, and in what countries?*"

ANSWER.—A few societies have spontaneously sprung up in Canada. Two have declared themselves auxiliary to the American. We have an agent—a native of the United States—in Upper Canada; not with a view to the organization of societies, but to the moral and intellectual elevation of the Ten thousand colored people there; most of whom have escaped from slavery in this Republic, to enjoy freedom under the protection of a Monarchy. In Great Britain there are numerous Anti-slavery Societies, whose particular object, of late, has been, to bring about the abolition of the Apprentice-system, as established by the emancipation act in her slaveholding colonies. In England, there is a society whose professed object is, to abolish slavery *throughout the world.* Of the existence of the British societies, you are, doubtless, fully aware ; as also of the fact, that, in Britain, the great mass of the people are opposed to slavery as it existed, a little while ago, in their own colonies, and as it exists now in the United States.— In France, the " French Society for the Abolition of Slavery" was founded in 1834. I shall have the pleasure of transmitting to you two pamphlets, containing an account of some of its proceedings ; from which you will learn, that, the Duc de Broglie is its presiding officer, and many of the most distinguished and influential of the public men of that country are members.—In Hayti, also, " The Haytian Abolition Society" was formed in May, 1836.

These are all the foreign societies of which I have knowledge. They are connected with the American by no formal affiliation. The only intercourse between them and it, is, that which springs up spontaneously among those of every land who sympathize with Humanity in her conflicts with Slavery.

" 4. *Do your or similar societies exist in the Colleges and other Literary institutions of the non-slaveholding states, and to what extent ?*"

Answer.—Strenuous efforts have been made, and they are still being made, by those who have the direction of most of the literary and theological institutions in the free states, to bar out our principles and doctrines, and prevent the formation of societies among the students. To this course they have been prompted by various, and possibly, in their view, good motives. One of them, I think it not uncharitable to say, is, to conciliate the wealthy of the south, that they may send their sons to the north, to swell the college catalogues. Neither do I think it uncharitable to say, that in this we have a manifestation of that Aristocratic pride, which, feeling itself honored by having entrusted to its charge the sons of distant, opulent, and distinguished planters, fails not to dull everything like sympathy for those whose unpaid toil supplies the means so lavishly expended in educating southern youth at northern colleges. These efforts at suppression or restraint, on the part of Faculties and Boards of Trustees, have heretofore succeeded to a considerable extent. Anti-Slavery Societies, notwithstanding, have been formed in a few of our most distinguished colleges and theological seminaries. Public opinion is beginning to call for a relaxation of restraints and impositions; they are yielding to its demands; and *now*, for the most part, sympathy for the slave may be manifested by our generous college youth, in the institution of Anti-Slavery Societies, without any downright prohibition by their more politic teachers. College societies will probably increase more rapidly hereafter; as, in addition to the removal or relaxation of former restraints, just referred to, the murder of Mr. Lovejoy, the assaults on the Freedom of speech and of the press, the prostration of the Right of petition in Congress, &c, &c, all believed to have been perpetrated to secure slavery from the scrutiny that the intelligent world is demanding, have greatly augmented the number of college abolitionists. They are, for the most part, the diligent, the intellectual, the religious of the students. United in societies, their influence is generally extensively felt in the surrounding region; *dispersed*, it seems scarcely less effective. An instance of the latter deserves particular notice.

The Trustees and Faculty of one of our theological and literary institutions united for the suppression of anti-slavery action among the students. The latter refused to cease pleading for the slave, as he could not plead for himself. They left the institution; were providentially dispersed over various parts of the country, and made useful, in a remarkable manner, in advancing the cause of humanity and liberty. One of these dismissed students, the son of a slaveholder, brought up in the midst of slavery, and well acquainted with its peculiarities, succeeded in persuading a pious father to emancipate his fourteen slaves. After lecturing a long time with signal success—having contracted a disease of the throat, which prevented him from further prosecuting his labors in this way—he visited the West Indies, eighteen months ago, in company with another gentleman of the most ample qualifications, to note the operation of the British emancipation act. Together, they collected a mass of facts—now in a course of publication—that will astonish, as it ought to delight, the whole south; for it shows, conclusively, that IMMEDIATE emancipation is the best, the safest, the most profitable, as it is the most just and honorable, of all emancipations.*

Another of these dismissed students is one of the secretaries of this society. He has, for a long time, discharged its arduous and responsi-

* See Appendix, A.

ble duties with singular ability. To his qualifications as secretary, he adds those of an able and successful lecturer. He was heard, several times, before the joint committee of the Legislature of Massachusetts, a year ago, prior to the report of that committee, and to the adoption, by the Senate and House of Representatives, of their memorable resolutions in favor of the Power of Congress to abolish slavery in the District of Columbia, and of the Right of petition.

" 5. *What do you estimate the number of those who co-operate in the matter at? What proportion do they bear in the population of the northern states, and what in the middle non-slaveholding states? Are they increasing, and at what rate?*"

ANSWER.—Those who stand *ready to join* our societies on the first suitable occasion, may be set down as equal in number to those who are now *actually members*. Those who are ready *fully to co-operate with us* in supporting the freedom of speech and the press, the right of petition, &c, may be estimated at *double*, if not *treble*, the joint numbers of those who *already are members*, and those who are *ready to become members*. The Recording secretary of the MASSACHUSETTS SOCIETY stated, a few weeks ago, that the abolitionists in the various minor societies in that state were one in thirty of the whole population. The proportion of abolitionists to the whole population is greater in Massachusetts than in any other of the free states, except VERMONT,-- where the spirit of liberty has almost entirely escaped the corruptions which slavery has infused into it in most of her sister states, by means of commercial and other intercourse with them.

In MAINE, not much of systematic effort has, as yet, been put forth to enlighten her population as to our principles and proceedings. I attended the anniversary of the State Society on the 31st of January, at Augusta, the seat of government. The Ministers of the large religious denominations were beginning, as I was told, to unite with us—and Politicians, to descry the ultimate prevalence of our principles. The impression I received was, that much could, and that much would, speedily be done.

In NEW HAMPSHIRE, more labor has been expended, and a greater effect produced. Public functionaries, who have been pleased to speak in contemptuous terms of the progress of abolitionism, both in Maine and New Hampshire, will, it is thought, soon be made to see, through a medium not at all deceptive, the grossness of their error.

In RHODE ISLAND, our principles are fast pervading the great body of the people. This, it is thought, is the only one of the free states, in

which the subject of abolition has been fully introduced, which has not
been disgraced by a mob, triumphant, for the time being, over the right
of the people to discuss any, and every, matter in which they feel interested.   A short time previous to the last election of members of Congress, questions, embodying our views as to certain political measures,
were propounded to the several candidates. Respectful answers,
and, in the main, conformable with our views, were returned.   I shall
transmit you a newspaper containing both the questions and the
answers.*

In CONNECTICUT, there has not been, as yet, a great expenditure of
abolition effort.   Although the moral tone of this state, so far as slavery
is concerned, has been a good deal weakened by the influence of her
multiform connexions with the south, yet the energies that have been
put forth to reanimate her ancient and lofty feelings, so far from proving
fruitless, have been followed by the most encouraging results. Evidence of this is found in the faithful administration of the laws by judges
and juries.   In May last, a slave, who had been brought from Georgia to
Hartford, successfully asserted her freedom under the laws of Connecticut.   The cause was elaborately argued before the Supreme
court.   The most eminent counsel were employed on both sides.
And it is but a few days, since two anti-abolition rioters (the only
ones on trial) were convicted before the Superior court in New
Haven, and sentenced to pay a fine of twenty dollars each, and
to be imprisoned six months, the longest term authorized by the law.
A convention, for the organization of a State Society, was held in the
city of Hartford on the last day of February.   It was continued three
days.   The *call* for it (which I send you) was signed by nearly EIGHTEEN
HUNDRED of the citizens of that state.   SEVENTEEN HUNDRED, as I was
informed, are legal voters.   The proceedings of the convention were
of the most harmonious and animating character.†

In NEW YORK, our cause is evidently advancing.   The state is rapidly coming up to the high ground of principle, so far as universal
liberty is concerned, on which the abolitionists would place her.   Several large Anti-Slavery conventions have lately been held in the western counties.   Their reports are of the most encouraging character.
Nor is the change more remarkable in the state than in this city.   Less
than five years ago, a few of the citizens advertised a meeting, to be

---

* Since the above was written, at the last election in this state for governor and lieutenant
governor, the abolitionists *interrogated* the gentlemen who stood candidates for these offices.
Two of them answered respectfully, and conformably to the views of the abolitionists. Their
opponents neglected to answer at all. The first were elected.—See Appendix, B.

† See Appendix, C.

held in Clinton Hall, to form a City Anti-Slavery Society. A mob prevented their assembling at the place appointed. They repaired, privately, to one of the churches. To this they were pursued by the mob, and routed from it, though not before they had completed, in a hasty manner, the form of organization. In the summer of 1834, some of the leading political and commercial journals of the city were enabled to stir up the mob against the persons and property of the abolitionists, and several of the most prominent were compelled to leave the city for safety; their houses were attacked, broken into, and, in one instance, the furniture publicly burnt in the street. *Now*, things are much changed. Many of the merchants and mechanics are favorable to our cause; gentlemen of the bar, especially the younger and more growing ones, are directing their attention to it; twenty-one of our city ministers are professed abolitionists; the churches are beginning to be more accessible to us; our meetings are held in them openly, attract large numbers, are unmolested; and the abolitionists sometimes hear themselves commended in other assemblies, not only for their honest *intentions*, but for their *respectability* and *intelligence*.

NEW JERSEY has, as yet, no State Society, and the number of avowed abolitionists is small. In some of the most populous and influential parts of the state, great solicitude exists on the subject; and the call for lecturers is beginning to be earnest, if not importunate.

PENNSYLVANIA has advanced to our principles just in proportion to the labor that has been bestowed, by means of lectures and publications in enlightening her population as to our objects, and the evils and dangers impending over the whole country, from southern slavery. The act of her late Convention, in depriving a large number of their own constituents (the colored people) of the elective franchise, heretofore possessed by them without any allegation of its abuse on their part, would seem to prove an unpropitious state of public sentiment. We would neither deny, nor elude, the force of such evidence. But when this measure of the convention is brought out and unfolded in its true light—shown to be a party measure to bring succor from the south— a mere following in the wake of North Carolina and Tennessee, who led the way, in their *new* constitutions, to this violation of the rights of their colored citizens, that they might the more firmly compact the wrongs of the enslaved—a pernicious, a profitless violation of great principles—a vulgar defiance of the advancing spirit of humanity and justice—a relapse into the by-gone darkness of a barbarous age—we apprehend from it no serious detriment to our cause.

OHIO has been well advanced. In a short time, she will be found among the most prominent of the states on the right side in the contest now going on between the spirit of liberty embodied in the free institutions of the north, and the spirit of slavery pervading the south. Her Constitution publishes the most honorable reprobation of slavery of any other in the Union. In providing for its own revision or amendment, it declares, that *no alteration of it shall ever take place, so as to introduce slavery or involuntary servitude into the state.* Her Supreme court is intelligent and firm. It has lately decided, virtually, against the constitutionality cf an act of the Legislature, made, in effect, to favor southern slavery by the persecution of the colored people within her bounds. She has, already, abolitionists enough to turn the scale in her elections, and an abundance of excellent material for augmenting the number.

In INDIANA but little has been done, except by the diffusion of our publications. But even with these appliances, several auxiliary societies have been organized.*

In MICHIGAN, the leaven of abolitionism pervades the whole population. The cause is well sustained by a high order of talent; and we trust soon to see the influence of it in all her public acts.

In ILLINOIS, the murder of Mr. Lovejoy has multiplied and confirmed abolitionists, and led to the formation of many societies, which, in all probability, would not have been formed so soon, had not that event taken place.

I am not possessed of sufficient data for stating, with precision, what proportion the abolitionists bear in the population of the Northern and Middle non-slaveholding states respectively. Within the last ten months, I have travelled extensively in both these geographical divisions I have had whatever advantage this, assisted by a strong interest in the general cause, and abundant conversations with the best informed abolitionists, could give, for making a fair estimate of their numbers. In the Northern states I should say, they are *one in ten*— in New York, New Jersey, and Pennsylvania, *one in twenty*—of the whole adult population. That the abolitionists have multiplied, and that they are still multiplying rapidly, no one acquainted with the smallness of their numbers at their first organization a few years ago, and who has kept his eyes about him since, need ask. That they have not, thus far, been more successful, is owing to the vastness of the undertaking, and the difficulties with which they have had to contend, from

---

* The first Legislative movement against the annexation of Texas to the Union, was made, it is believed, in Indiana. So early as December, 1836, a joint resolution passed its second reading in one or both branches of the Legislature. How it was ultimately disposed of, is not known.

comparatively limited means, for presenting their measures and objects, with the proper developments and explanations, to the great mass of the popular mind. The progress of their principles, under the same amount of intelligence in presenting them, and where no peculiar causes of prejudice exist in the minds of the hearers, is generally proportioned to the degree of religious and intellectual worth prevailing in the different sections of the country where the subject is introduced. I know no instance, in which any one notoriously profane or intemperate, or licentious, or of openly irreligious *practice*, has professed, cordially to have received our principles.

" 6. *What is the object your associations aim at? Does it extend to abolition of slavery only in the District of Columbia, or in the whole slave country ?*"

ANSWER.—This question is fully answered in the second Article of the Constitution of the American Anti-Slavery Society, which is in these words :—

" The object of this society is the entire abolition of slavery in the United States. While it admits that each state, in which slavery exists, has, by the Constitution of the United States, the exclusive right to *legislate* in regard to its abolition in said state, it shall aim to convince all our fellow-citizens, by arguments addressed to their understandings and consciences, that slaveholding is a heinous crime in the sight of God, and that the duty, safety, and best interests of all concerned require its immediate abandonment, without expatriation. The society will also endeavor, in a constitutional way, to influence Congress to put an end to the domestic slave-trade, and to abolish slavery in all those portions of our common country which come under its control, especially in the District of Columbia ; and likewise to prevent the extension of it to any state that may hereafter be admitted to the Union."

Other objects, accompanied by a pledge of peace, are stated in the third article of the Constitution,—

" This Society shall aim to elevate the character and condition of the people of color, by encouraging their intellectual, moral, and religious improvement, and by removing public prejudice,—that thus they may, according to their intellectual and moral worth, share an equality with the whites of civil and religious privileges ; but this Society will never in any way, countenance the oppressed in vindicating their rights by resorting to physical force."

" 7. *By what means and by what power do you propose to carry your views into effect ?*"

ANSWER.—Our "means" are the Truth,—the "Power" under whose guidance we propose to carry our views into effect, is, the Almighty. Confiding in these means, when directed by the spirit and wisdom of Him, who has so made them as to act on the hearts of men, and so constituted the hearts of men as to be affected by them, we expect, 1. To bring the CHURCH of this country to repentance for the sin of OPPRESSION. Not only the Southern portion of it that has been the oppressor —but the Northern, that has stood by, consenting, for half a century, to the wrong. 2. To bring our countrymen to see, that for a nation to persist in injustice is, but to rush on its own ruin; that to do justice is the highest expediency—to love mercy its noblest ornament. In other countries, slavery has sometimes yielded to fortuitous circumstances, or been extinguished by physical force. *We* strive to win for truth the victory over error, and on the broken fragments of slavery to rear for her a temple, that shall reach to the heavens, and toward which all nations shall worship. It has been said, that the slaveholders of the South will not yield, nor hearken to the influence of the truth on this subject. We believe it not—nor give we entertainment to the slander that such an unworthy defence of them implies. We believe them *men*,—that they have understandings that arguments will convince—consciences to which the appeals of justice and mercy will not be made in vain. If our principles be true—our arguments right—if slaveholders be men— and God have not delivered over our guilty country to the retributions of the oppressor, not only of the STRANGER but of the NATIVE—our success is certain.

" 8. *What has been for three years past, the annual income of your societies? And how has it been raised?*

ANSWER.—The annual income of the societies at large, it would be impossible to ascertain. The total receipts of this society, for the year ending 9th of May, 1835—leaving out odd numbers—was $10,000; for the year ending 9th of May, 1837, $25,000; and for the year ending 11th of May, 1836, $38,000. From the last date, up to this—not quite ten months—there has been paid into the treasury the sum of $36,000.* These sums are independent of what is raised by state and auxiliary societies, for expenditure within their own particular bounds, and for their own particular exigencies. Also, of the sums paid in subscriptions for the support of newspapers, and for the printing (by auxiliaries,) of periodicals, pamphlets, and essays, either for sale at low

* The report for May states the sum received, during the previous year, at $44,000.

prices, or for gratuitous distribution. The moneys contributed in these various modes would make an aggregate greater, perhaps, than is paid into the treasury of any one of the Benevolent societies of the country. Most of the wealthy contributors of former years suffered so severely in the money-pressure of this, that they have been unable to contribute much to our funds. This has made it necessary to call for aid on the great body of abolitionists—persons, generally, in moderate circumstances. They have well responded to the call, considering the hardness of the times. To show you the extremes that meet at our treasury,—General Sewall, of Maine, a revolutionary officer, eighty-five years old—William Philbrick, a little boy near Boston, not four years old—and a colored woman, who makes her subsistence by selling apples in the streets in this city, lately sent in their respective sums to assist in promoting the emancipation of the "poor slave."

All contributions of whatever kind are *voluntary.*

" 9. *In what way, and to what purposes do you apply these funds !*"

Answer.—They are used in sustaining the society's office in this city—in paying lecturers and agents of various kinds—in upholding the press—in printing books, pamphlets, tracts, &c, containing expositions of our principles—accounts of our progress—refutations of objections —and disquisitions on points, scriptural, constitutional, political, legal, economical, as they chance to arise and become important. In this office three secretaries are employed in different departments of duty ; one editor ; one publishing agent, with an assistant, and two or three young men and boys, for folding, directing, and despatching papers, executing errands, &c. The business of the society has increased so much of late, as to make it necessary, in order to ensure the proper despatch of it, to employ additional clerks for the particular exigency. Last year, the society had in its service about sixty "permanent agents." This year, the number is considerably diminished, The deficiency has been more than made up by creating a large number of " Local" agents—so called, from the fact, that being generally Professional men, lawyers or physicians in good practice, or Ministers with congregations, they are confined, for the most part, to their respective neighborhoods. Some of the best minds in our country are thus engaged. Their labors have not only been eminently successful, but have been rendered at but small charge to the society ; they receiving only their travelling expenses, whilst employed in lecturing and forming societies. In the case of a minister, there is the additional expense of supplying his pulpit while absent on the business of his agency, However, in many instances, these agents, being in easy circumstances, make no charge, even for their expenses.

In making appointments, the executive committee have no regard to party discrimination. This will be fully understood, when it is stated, that on a late occasion, two of our local agents were the candidates of their respective political parties for the office of Secretary of State for the state of Vermont.

It ought to be stated here, that two of the most effective advocates of the anti-slavery cause are females—the Misses Grimké—natives of South Carolina—brought up in the midst of the usages of slavery—most intelligently acquainted with the merits of the system, and qualified, in an eminent degree, to communicate their views to others in public addresses. They are not only the advocates of the slave at their own charge, but they actually contribute to the funds of the societies, So successfully have they recommended the cause of emancipation to the crowds that attended their lectures during the last year, that they were permitted on three several occasions publicly to address the joint committee (on slavery) of the Massachusetts Legislature, now in session, on the interesting matters that occupy their attention.

"10 *How many printing-presses and periodical publications have you?*

ANSWER.—We own no press. Our publications are all printed by contract. The EMANCIPATOR and HUMAN RIGHTS are the organs of the Executive Committee. The first (which you have seen,) is a large sheet, is published weekly, and employs almost exclusively the time of the gentleman who edits it. Human Rights is a monthly sheet of smaller size, and is edited by one of the secretaries. The increasing interest that is fast manifesting itself in the cause of emancipation and its kindred subjects will, in all probability, before long, call for the more frequent publication of one or both of these papers.—The ANTI-SLAVE-RY MAGAZINE, a quarterly, was commenced in October, 1835, and continued through two years. It has been intermitted, only to make the necessary arrangements for issuing it on a more extended scale.—It is proposed to give it size enough to admit the amplest discussions that we or our opponents may desire, and to give *them* a full share of its room—in fine, to make it, in form and merit, what the importance of the subject calls for. I send you a copy of the Prospectus for the new series.—The ANTI-SLAVERY RECORD, published for three years as a monthly, has been discontinued *as such*, and it will be issued hereafter, only as occasion may require.—THE SLAVE'S FRIEND, a small monthly tract, of neat appearance, intended principally for children and young persons, has been issued for several years. It is replete with facts relating to slavery, and with accounts of the hair-breadth escapes of slaves from their masters and pursuers that rarely fail to impart the most thrilling interest to its little readers.—Besides these, there is the ANTI-SLAVERY EXAMINER, in which are published, as the times call for them, our larger essays partaking of a controversial character, such as Smith's reply to the Rev. Mr. Smylie—Grimké's letter and " Wythe." By turning to page 32 of our Fourth Report (included in your order for books, &c,) you will find, that in the year ending 11th May, the issues from the press were—bound volumes, 7,877—Tracts and Pamphlets, 47,250—Circulars, &c, 4,100—Prints, 10,490—Anti-Slavery Magazine, 9000—Slave's Friend, 131,050—Human Rights, 189,400—Emancipator, 217,000. These are the issues of the American Anti-Slavery Society, from their office in this city. Other publications of similar character are issued by State Societies or individuals —the LIBERATOR, in Boston; HERALD OF FREEDOM, in Concord, N. H.; ZION'S WATCHMAN and the COLORED AMERICAN in this city. The latter is conducted in the editorial, and other departments, by colored citizens. You can judge of its character, by a few numbers that I send to you. Then, there is the FRIEND OF MAN, in Utica, in this state. The NATIONAL ENQUIRER, in Philadelphia;* the CHRISTIAN WITNESS, in Pittsburgh; the PHILANTHROPIST, in Cincinnati.—All these are sustained by the friends, and devoted almost exclusively to the cause, of emancipation. Many of the Religious journals that do not make emancipation their main object have adopted the sentiments of abolitionists, and aid in promoting them. The Alton Observer, edited by the late Mr. Lovejoy, was one of these.

From the data I have, I set down the newspapers, as classed above, at upwards of one hundred. Here it may also be stated, that the presses which print the abolition journals above named, throw off besides, a great variety of other anti-slavery matter, in the form of books, pamphlets, single sheets, &c, &c, and that, at many of the principal commercial points throughout the free states, DEPOSITORIES are established, at which our publications of every sort are kept for sale. A large and fast increasing number of the Political journals of the country have become, within the last two years, if not the avowed supporters of our cause, well inclined to it. Formerly, it was a common thing for most of the leading *party*-papers, especially in the large cities, to

* The NATIONAL ENQUIRER, edited by Benjamin Lundy, has been converted into the PENNSYL- VANIA FREEMAN, edited by John G. Whittier. Mr. Lundy proposes to issue the GENIUS OF UNI- VERSAL EMANCIPATION, in Illinois.

speak of the abolitionists in terms signally disrespectful and offensive. Except in rare instances, and these, it is thought, only where they are largely subsidized by southern patronage, it is not so now. The desertions that are taking place from their ranks will, in a short time, render their position undesirable for any, who aspire to gain, or influence, or reputation in the North.

" 11. *To what class of persons do you address your publications—and are they addressed to the judgment, the imagination, or the feelings?*"

ANSWER.—They are intended for the great mass of intelligent mind, both in the free and in the slave states. They partake, of course, of the intellectual peculiarities of the different authors. Jay's "INQUIRY" and Mrs. Child's " APPEAL" abound in facts—are dispassionate, ingenious, argumentative. The " BIBLE AGAINST SLAVERY," by the most careful and laborious research, has struck from slavery the prop, which careless Annotators, (writing, unconscious of the influence, the prevailing system of slavery throughout the Christian world exercised on their own minds,) have admitted was furnished for it in the Scriptures. " Wythe" by a pains-taking and lucid adjustment of facts in the history of the Government, both before and after the adoption of the Constitution, and with a rigor of logic, that cannot, it is thought, be successfully encountered, has put to flight forever with unbiased minds, every doubt as to the " Power of Congress over the District of Columbia."

There are among the abolitionists, Poets, and by the acknowledgment of their opponents, poets of no mean name too—who, as the use of poets is, do address themselves often—as John G. Whittier does *always*—powerfully to the imagination and feelings of their readers.

Our publications cannot be classed according to any particular style or quality of composition. They may characterized generally, as well suited to affect the public mind—to rouse into healthful activity the conscience of this nation, stupified, torpid, almost dead, in relation to HUMAN RIGHTS, the high theme of which they treat!

It has often been alleged, that our writings appeal to the worst passions of the slaves, and that they are placed in their hands with a view to stir them to revolt. Neither charge has any foundation in truth to rest upon. The first finds no support in the tenor of the writings themselves ; the last ought forever to be abandoned, in the absence of any single well authenticated instance of their having been conveyed by abolitionists to slaves, or of their having been even found in their possession. To instigate the slaves to revolt, as the means of obtaining their liberty, would prove a lack of wisdom and honesty that none would

impute to abolitionists, except such as are unacquainted with their character. Revolt would be followed by the sure destruction, not only of
all the slaves who might be concerned in it, but of multitudes of the
innocent. Moreover, the abolitionists, as a class, are religious—they
favor peace, and stand pledged in their constitution, before the country
and heaven, to abide in peace, so far as a forcible vindication of the right
of the slaves to their freedom is concerned. Further still, no small
number of them deny the right of defence, either to individuals or nations,
even when forcibly and wrongfully attacked. This disagreement among
ourselves on this single point—of which our adversaries are by no
means ignorant, as they often throw it reproachfully in our teeth—would
forever prevent concert in any scheme that looked to instigating servile
revolt. If there be, in all our ranks, one, who—personal danger out of
the question—would excite the slaves to insurrection and massacre,
or who would not be swift to reveal the earliest attempt to concoct
such an iniquity—I say, on my obligations as a man, he is unknown
to me.

Yet it ought not to be matter of surprise to abolitionists, that the South
should consider them "fanatics," "incendiaries," "cut-throats," and
call them so too. The South has had their character reported to them
by the North, by those who are their neighbors, who, it was supposed,
knew, and would speak the truth, and the truth only, concerning them.
It would, I apprehend, be unavailing for abolitionists now to enter on
any formal vindication of their character from charges that can be so
easily repeated after every refutation. False and fraudulent as they
know them to be, they must be content to live under them till the con-
summation of the work of Freedom shall prove to the master that they
have been *his* friends, as well as the friends of the slave. The mis-
chief of these charges has fallen on the South—the malice is to be
placed to the credit of the North.

" 12. *Do you propagate your doctrines by any other means than oral and
written discussions—for instance, by prints and pictures in manufactures—
say of pocket-handkerchiefs, calicoes, &c ? Pray, state the various modes ?"*

ANSWER.—Two or three years ago, an abolitionist of this city pro-
cured to be manufactured, at his own charge, a small lot of children's
pocket-handkerchiefs, impressed with anti-slavery pictures and mottoes. I have no recollection of having seen any of them but once.
None such, I believe, are now to be found, or I would send you a sam-
ple. If any manufactures of the kinds mentioned, or others similar to
them, are in existence, they have been produced independently of the

agency of this society. It is thought that none such exist, unless the following should be supposed to fall within the terms of the inquiry. Female abolitionists often unite in sewing societies. They meet together, usually once a week or fortnight, and labor through the afternoon, with their own hands, to furnish means for advancing the cause of the slave. One of the company reads passages from the Bible, or some religious book, whilst the others are engaged at their work. The articles they prepare, especially if they be of the "fancy" kind, are often ornamented with handsomely executed emblems, underwritten with appropriate mottoes. The picture of a slave kneeling (such as you will see impressed on one of the sheets of this letter) and supplicating in the words, "AM I NOT A MAN AND A BROTHER," is an example. The mottoes or sentences are, however, most generally selected from the Scriptures; either appealing to human sympathy in behalf of human suffering, or breathing forth God's tender compassion for the oppressed, or proclaiming, in thunder tones, his avenging justice on the oppressor. A few quotations will show their general character : -

"Blessed is he that considereth the poor."

"Defend the poor and fatherless ; do justice to the afflicted and needy. Deliver the poor and the needy ; rid him out of the hand of the wicked."

"Open thy mouth for the dumb, plead the cause of the poor and needy."

"Blessed are the merciful, for they shall obtain mercy."

"First, be reconciled to thy brother, and then come and offer thy gift."

"Thou shalt love thy neighbor as thyself."

"All things whatsoever ye would that men should do to you, do ye even so to them."

Again :—

"For he shall deliver the needy when he crieth ; the poor also, and him that hath no helper."

"The Lord looseth the prisoners ; the Lord raiseth them that are bowed down ; the Lord preserveth the strangers."

"He hath sent me to heal the broken-hearted, to preach deliverance to the captives, to set at liberty them that are bruised."

"For the oppression of the poor, for the sighing of the needy, now will I arise, saith the Lord ; I will set him in safety from him that puffeth at him."

Again :—

"The Lord executeth righteousness and judgment for all that are oppressed."

"Rob not the poor because he is poor, neither oppress the afflicted in the gate ; for the Lord will plead their cause, and spoil the soul of those that spoiled them."

"And I will come near to you to judgment, and I will be a swift witness against those that oppress the hireling in his wages, the widow and the fatherless, and that turn aside the stranger from his right, and fear not me, saith the Lord of hosts."

"Wo unto him that buildeth his house by unrighteousness, and his chambers by wrong ; that useth his neighbor's service without wages, and giveth him not for his work "

Fairs, for the sale of articles fabricated by the hands of female abolitionists, and recommended by such pictures and sentences as those quoted above, are held in many of our cities and large towns. Crowds frequent them to purchase ; hundreds of dollars are thus realized, to be appropriated to the anti-slavery cause ; and, from the cheap rate at which the articles are sold, vast numbers of them are scattered far and wide over the country. Besides these, if we except various drawings or pictures on *paper*, (samples of which were put up in the packages you ordered a few days ago,) such as the Slave-market in the District of Columbia, with Members of congress attending it—views of slavery in the South—a Lynch court in the slave-states—the scourging of Mr. Dresser by a vigilance committee in the public square of Nashville—the plundering of the post-office in Charleston, S. C., and the conflagration of part of its contents, &c, &c, I am apprised of no other means of propagating our doctrines than by oral and written discussions.

" 13. *Are your hopes and expectations of success increased or lessened by the events of the last year, and especially by the action of this Congress? And will your exertions be relaxed or increased ?*

ANSWER.— The events of the last year, including the action of the present Congress, are of the same character with the events of the eighteen months which immediately preceded it. In the question before us, they may be regarded as one series. I would say, answering your interrogatory generally, that none of them, however unpropitious to the cause of the abolitionists they may appear, to those who look at the subject from an opposite point to the one *they* occupy, seem, thus far, in any degree to have lessened their hopes and expectations The events alluded to have not come altogether unexpected. They are regarded as the legitimate manifestations of slavery—necessary, perhaps, in the present dull and unapprehensive state of the public mind as to human rights, to be brought out and spread before the people, before they will sufficiently revolt against slavery itself.

1. They are seen in the CHURCH, and in the practice of its individual members. The southern portion of the American church may now be regarded as having admitted the dogma, that *slavery is a Divine institution*. She has been forced by the anti-slavery discussion into this position—either to cease from slaveholding, or formally to adopt the only alternative, that slaveholding is right. She has chosen the alternative—reluctantly, to be sure, but substantially, and, within the last year, almost unequivocally. In defending what was dear to her, she has been forced

to cast away her garments, and thus to reveal a deformity, of which she herself, before, was scarcely aware, and the existence of which others did not credit. So much for the action of the southern church as a body.—On the part of her MEMBERS, the revelation of a time-serving spirit, that not only yielded to the ferocity of the multitude, but fell in with it, may be reckoned among the events of the last three years. Instances of this may be found in the attendance of the " clergy of all denominations," at a tumultuous meeting of the citizens of Charleston, S. C., held in August, 1835, for the purpose of reducing to *system* their unlawful surveillance and control of the post-office and mail; and in the alacrity with which they obeyed the popular call to dissolve the Sunday-schools for the instruction of the colored people. Also in the fact, that, throughout the whole South, church members are not only found on the Vigilance Committees, (tribunals organized in opposition to the laws of the states where they exist,) but uniting with the merciless and the profligate in passing sentence consigning to infamous and excruciating, if not extreme punishment, persons, by their own acknowledgment, innocent of any unlawful act. Out of sixty persons that composed the vigilance committee which condemned Mr. Dresser to be scourged in the public square of Nashville, TWENTY-SEVEN were members of churches, and one of them a professed Teachers of Christianity. A member of the committee stated afterward, in a newspaper of which he was the editor, that Mr. D. *had not laid himself liable to any punishment known to the laws.* Another instance is to be found in the conduct of the Rev. Wm. S. Plumer, of Virginia. Having been absent from Richmond, when the ministers of the gospel assembled together formally to testify their abhorrence of the abolitionists, he addressed the chairman of the committee of correspondence a note, in which he uses this language :—" If abolitionists will set the country in a blaze, it is but fair that they should have the first warming at the fire."—" Let them understand, that they will be caught, if they come among us, and they will take good heed to keep out of our way." Mr. P. has no doubtful standing in the Presbyterian church with which he is connected. He has been regarded as one of its brightest ornaments.* To drive the slaveholding church and its members from the equivocal, the neutral position, from which they had so long successfully defended slavery— to compel them to elevate their practice to an even height with their avowed principles, or to degrade their principles to the level of their known practice, was a preliminary, necessary in the view of abo-

---

*In the division of the General Assembly of the Presbyterian church, that has just taken place, Mr. Plumer has been elected Moderator of the " Old School" portion.

litionists, either for bringing that part of the church into the common action against slavery, or as a ground for treating it as confederate with oppressors. So far, then, as the action of the church, or of its individual members, is to be reckoned among the events of the last two or three years, the abolitionists find in it nothing to lessen their hopes or expectations

2. The abolitionists believed, from the beginning, that the slaves of the South were (as slaves are everywhere) unhappy, *because of their condition.* Their adversaries denied it, averring that, as a class, they were "contented and happy." The abolitionists thought that the argument against slavery could be made good, so far as this point was concerned, by either *admitting* or *denying* the assertion.

Admitting it, they insisted, that, nothing could demonstrate the turpitude of any system more surely than the fact, that MAN—made in the image of God—but a little lower than the angels—crowned with glory and honor, and set over the works of God's hands—his mind sweeping in an instant from planet to planet, from the sun of one system to the sun of another, even to the great centre sun of them all—contemplating the machinery of the universe "wheeling unshaken" in the awful and mysterious grandeur of its movements "through the void immense"— with a spirit delighting in upward aspiration—bounding from earth to heaven—that seats itself fast by the throne of God, to drink in the instructions of Infinite Wisdom, or flies to execute the commands of Infinite Goodness;—that such a being could be made "contented and happy" with "enough to eat, and drink, and wear," and shelter from the weather—with the base provision that satisfies the brutes, is (say the abolitionists) enough to render superfluous all other arguments for the *instant* abandonment of a system whose appropriate work is such infinite wrong.

Denying that "the slaves are contented and happy," the abolitionists have argued, that, from the structure of his moral nature—the laws of his mind—man cannot be happy in the fact, that he is *enslaved.* True, he may be happy in slavery, but it is not slavery that makes him so— it is virtue and faith, elevating him above the afflictions of his lot. The slave has a will, leading him to seek those things which the Author of his nature has made conducive to its happiness. In these things, the will of the master comes in collision with his will. The slave desires to receive the rewards of his own labor; the power of the master wrests them from him. The slave desires to possess his wife, to whom God has joined him, in affection, to have the superintendence, and enjoy the services, of the children whom God has confided to him as a parent

4

to train them, by the habits of the filial relation, for the yet higher relation that they may sustain to him as their heavenly Father. But here he is met by the opposing will of the master, pressing *his* claims with irresistible power. The ties that heaven has sanctioned and blessed—of husband and wife, of parent and child—are all sundered in a moment by the master, at the prompting of avarice or luxury or lust; and there is none that can stay his ruthless hand, or say unto him, " What doest thou ?" The slave thirsts for the pleasures of refined and elevated intellect—the master denies to him the humblest literary acquisition. The slave pants to know something of that still higher nature that he feels burning within him—of his present state, his future destiny, of the Being who made him, to whose judgment-seat he is going. The master's interests cry, " No !" " Such knowledge is too wonderful for you ; it is high, you cannot attain unto it." To predicate *happiness* of a class of beings, placed in circumstances where their will is everlastingly defeated by an irresistible power—the abolitionists say, is to prove them destitute of the sympathies of *our* nature—not *human*. It is to declare with the Atheist, that man is independent of the goodness of his Creator for his enjoyments—that human happiness calls not for any of the appliances of his bounty—that God's throne is a nullity, himself a superfluity.

But, independently of any abstract reasoning drawn from the nature of moral and intelligent beings, FACTS have been elicited in the discussion of the point before us, proving slavery everywhere (especially Southern slavery, maintained by enlightened Protestants of the nineteenth century) replete with torments and horrors—the direst form of oppression that upheaves itself before the sun. These facts have been so successfully impressed on a large portion of the intelligent mind of the country, that the slaves of the South are beginning to be considered as those whom God emphatically regards as the " poor," the " needy," the " afflicted," the " oppressed," the " bowed down ;" and for whose consolation he has said, " Now will I arise—I will set him in safety from him that puffeth at him."

This state of the public mind has been brought about within the last two or three years ; and it is an event which, so far from lessening, greatly animates, the hopes and expectations of abolitionists.

3. The abolitionists believed from the first, that the tendency of slavery is to produce, on the part of the whites, looseness of morals, disdain of the wholesome restraints of law, and a ferocity of temper, found, only in solitary instances, in those countries where slavery is unknown. They were not ignorant of the fact, that this was disputed ; nor that

the " CHIVALRY OF THE SOUTH" had become a cant phrase, including
all that is high-minded and honorable among men ; nor, that it had been
formally asserted in our National legislature, that slavery, as it exists
in the South, " produces the highest toned, the purest, best organization
of society that has ever existed on the face of the earth." Nor were
the abolitionists unaware, that these pretensions, proving anything else
but their own solidity, had been echoed and re-echoed so long by the
unthinking and the interested of the North, that the character of the
South had been injuriously affected by them—till she began boldly to
attribute her *peculiar* superiority to her *peculiar* institution, and thus to
strengthen it. All this the abolitionists saw and knew. But few others
saw and understood it as they did. The revelations of the last three
years are fast dissipating the old notion, and bringing multitudes in the
North to see the subject as the abolitionists see it. When " Southern
Chivalry" and the *purity* of southern society are spoken of now, it is at
once replied, that a large number of the slaves show, by their *color*, their
indisputable claim to white paternity ; and that, notwithstanding their
near consanguineous relation to the whites, they are still held and treated, in all respects, *as slaves.* Nor is it forgotten now, when the claims
of the South to " hospitality" are pressed, to object, because they are
grounded on the unpaid wages of the laborer—on the robbery of the
poor. When " Southern generosity" is mentioned, the old adage, " be
just before you are generous," furnishes the reply. It is no proof of
generosity (say the objectors) to take the bread of the laborer, to lavish
it in banquetings on the rich. When " Southern Chivalry" is the theme
of its admirers, the hard-handed, but intelligent, working man of the
North asks, if the espionage of southern hotels, and of ships and steam-
boats on their arrival at southern ports ; if the prowl, by day and by
night, for the solitary stranger suspected of sympathizing with the
enslaved, that he may be delivered over to the mercies of a vigilance
committee, furnishes the proof of its existence ; if the unlawful importation of slaves from Africa* furnishes the proof ; if the abuse, the
scourging, the hanging on suspicion, without law, of friendless stran-

* Mr. Mercer, of Virginia, some years ago, asserted in Congress, that " CARGOES" of African
slaves were smuggled into the southern states to a deplorable extent. Mr. Middleton, of South
Carolina, declared it to be his belief, that THIRTEEN THOUSAND Africans were annually smuggled
into the southern states. Mr. Wright, of Maryland, estimated the number at FIFTEEN THOUSAND.
Miss Martineau was told in 1835, by a wealthy slaveholder of Louisiana, (who probably spoke of
that state alone,) that the annual importation of native Africans was from THIRTEEN THOUSAND
to FIFTEEN THOUSAND. The President of the United States, in his last Annual Message, speaking of the Navy, says, " The large force under Commodore Dallas [on the West India station] has
been most actively and efficiently employed in protecting our commerce, IN PREVENTING THE
IMPORTATION OF SLAVES, &c."

gers, furnish the proof; if the summary execution of slaves and of colored freemen, almost by the score, without legal trial, furnishes the proof; if the cruelties and tortures to which *citizens* have been exposed, and the burning to death of slaves by slow fires,* furnish the proof. All these things, says he, furnish any thing but proof of *true* hospitality, or generosity, or gallantry, or purity, or chivalry.

Certain it is, that the time when southern slavery derived countenance at the North, from its supposed connection with " chivalry," is rapidly passing away. " Southern Chivalry" will soon be regarded as one of the by-gone fooleries of a less intelligent and less virtuous age. It will soon be cast out—giving place to the more reasonable idea, that the denial of wages to the laborer, the selling of men and women, the whipping of husbands and wives in each others presence, to compel them to unrequited toil, the deliberate attempt to extinguish mind, and, consequently, to destroy the soul—is among the highest offences against God and man—unspeakably mean and ungentlemanly.

The impression made on the minds of the people as to this matter, is one of the events of the last two or three years that does not contribute to lessen the hopes or expectations of abolitionists.

4. The ascendency that Slavery has acquired, and exercises, in the administration of the government, and the apprehension now prevailing among the sober and intelligent, irrespective of party, that it will soon overmaster the Constitution itself, may be ranked among the events of the last two or three years that affect the course of abolitionists. The abolitionists regard the Constitution with unabated affection. They hold in no common veneration the memory of those who made it. They would be the last to brand Franklin and King and Morris and Wilson and Sherman and Hamilton with the ineffaceable infamy of attempting to ingraft on the Constitution, and therefore to *perpetuate*, a system of oppression in absolute antagonism to its high and professed objects, one which their own practice condemned,—and this, too, when they had scarcely wiped away the dust and sweat of the Revolution from their brows! Whilst abolitionists feel and speak thus of our Constitutional fathers, they do not justify the dereliction of principle into which they were betrayed, when they imparted to the work of their hands *any* power to contribute to the continuance of such a system. They can only palliate it, by supposing, that they thought, slavery was already a waning institution, destined soon to pass away. In their time, (1787) slaves were

* Within the last few years, four slaves, and one citizen of color, have been put to death in this manner, in Alabama, Mississippi, Missouri, and Arkansas.

comparatively of little value—there being then no great slave-labor staple (as cotton is now) to make them profitable to their holders.* Had the circumstances of the country remained as they then were, slave-labor, always and every where the most expensive—would have disappeared before the competition of free labour. They had seen, too, the principle of universal liberty, on which the Revolution was justified, recognised and embodied in most of the State Constitutions ; they had seen slavery utterly forbidden in that of Vermont—instantaneously abolished in that of Massachusetts—and laws enacted in the New-England States and in Pennsylvania, for its gradual abolition. Well might they have anti-cipated, that Justice and Humanity, now starting forth with fresh vigor, would, in their march, sweep away the whole system ; more especially, as freedom of speech and of the press—the legitimate abolisher not only of the acknowledged vice of slavery, but of every other that time should reveal in our institutions or practices—had been fully secured to the people. Again ; power was conferred on Congress to put a stop to the African slave-trade, without which it was thought, at that time, to be impossible to maintain slavery, as a system, on this continent,—so great was the havoc it committed on human life. Authority was also granted to Congress to prevent the transfer of slaves, as articles of commerce, from one State to another ; and the introduction of slavery into the terri-tories. All this was crowned by the power of refusing admission into the Union, to any new state, whose form of government was repugnant to the principles of liberty set forth in that of the United States. The faithful execution, by Congress, of these powers, it was reason-ably enough supposed, would, at least, prevent the growth of slavery, if it did not entirely remove it. Congress did, at the set time, execute *one* of them—deemed, then, the most effectual of the whole ; but, as it has turned out, the least so.

The effect of the interdiction of the African slave-trade was, not to diminish the trade itself, or greatly to mitigate its horrors ; it only changed its name from African to American—transferred the seat of commerce from Africa to America—its profits from African princes to American farmers. Indeed, it is almost certain, if the African slave-trade had been left unrestrained, that slavery would not have covered so large a portion of our country as it does now. The cheap rate at which slaves might have been imported by the planters of the south, would have prevented the rearing of them for sale, by the farmers of

* The cultivation of cotton was almost unknown in the United States before 1787. It was not till two years afterward that it began to be raised or exported. (See Report of the Secretary of the Treasury, Feb. 29, 1836.)—See Appendix, D.

Maryland, Virginia, and the other slave-selling states. If these states could be 'restrained from the *commerce* in slaves, slavery could not be supported by them for any length of time, or to any considerable extent. They could not maintain it, as an economical system, under the competition of free labor. It is owing to the *non-user* by Congress, or rather to their unfaithful application of their power to the other points, on which it was expected to act for the limitation or extermination of slavery, that the hopes of our fathers have not been realized ; and that slavery has, at length, become so audacious, as openly to challenge the principles of 1776—to trample on the most precious rights secured to the citizen—to menace the integrity of the Union and the very existence of of the government itself.

Slavery has advanced to its present position by steps that were, at first, gradual, and, for a long time, almost unnoticed ; afterward, it made its way by intimidating or corrupting those who ought to have been forward to resist its pretensions. Up to the time of the " Missouri Compromise," by which the nation was wheedled out of its honor, slavery was looked on as an evil that was finally to yield to the expanding and ripening influences of our Constitutional principles and regulations. Why it has not yielded, we may easily see, by even a slight glance at some of the incidents in our history.

It has already been said, that we have been brought into our present condition by the unfaithfulness of Congress, in not *exerting* the power vested in it, to stop the domestic slave-trade, and in the *abuse* of the power of admitting " *new* states" into the Union. Kentucky made application in 1792, with a slave-holding Constitution in her hand.—With what a mere *technicality* Congress suffered itself to be drugged into torpor :—*She was part of one of the " Original States"—and therefore entitled to all their privileges.*

One precedent established, it was easy to make another. Tennessee was admitted in 1796, without scruple, on the same ground.

The next triumph of slavery was in 1803, in the purchase of Louisiana, acknowledged afterward, even by Mr. Jefferson who made it, to be unauthorized by the Constitution—and in the establishment of slavery throughout its vast limits, actually and substantially under the auspices of that instrument which declares its only objects to be—" to form a more perfect union, establish JUSTICE, insure DOMESTIC TRANQUILITY, provide for the common defence, promote the general welfare, and secure the blessings of LIBERTY to ourselves and our posterity"*

---

* It may be replied, The colored people were held as *property* by the laws of Louisiana previously to the cession, and that Congress had no right to divest the newly acquired citizens of their pro

In this case, the violation of the Constitution was suffered to pass with but little opposition, except from Massachusetts, because we were content to receive in exchange, multiplied commercial benefits and enlarged territorial limits.

The next stride that slavery made over the Constitution was in the admission of the State of Louisiana into the Union. *She* could claim no favor as part of an " Original State." At this point, it might have been supposed, the friends of Freedom and of the Constitution according to its original intent, would have made a stand. But no : with the exception of Massachusetts, they hesitated and were persuaded to acquiesce, because the country was just about entering into a war with England, and the crisis was unpropitious for discussing questions that would create divisions between different sections of the Union. We must wait till the country was at peace. Thus it was that Louisiana was admitted without a controversy.

Next followed, in 1817 and 1820, Mississippi and Alabama—admitted after the example of Kentucky and Tennessee, without any contest.

Meantime, Florida had given some uneasiness to the slaveholders of the neighboring states ; and for their accommodation chiefly, a negociation was set on foot by the government to purchase it.

Missouri was next in order in 1821. She could plead no privilege, on the score of being part of one of the original states ; the country too, was relieved from the pressure of her late conflict with England ; it was prosperous and quiet ; every thing seemed propitious to a calm and dispassionate consideration of the claims of slaveholders to add props to their system, by admitting indefinitely, new slave states to the Union. Up to this time, the " EVIL" of slavery had been almost universally acknowledged and deplored by the South, and its termination (apparently) sincerely hoped for.* By this management its friends

---

perty. This statement is evasive. It does not include, nor touch the question, which is this :—Had Congress, or the treaty-making power, a right to recognise, and, by recognising, to establish, in a territory that had no claim of privilege, on the ground of being part of one of the " Original States," a condition of things that it could not establish *directly*, because there was no grant in the constitution of power, direct or incidental, to do so—and because, *to do so*, was in downright oppugnancy to the principles of the Constitution itself? The question may be easily answered by stating the following case :—Suppose a law had existed in Louisiana, previous to the cession, by which the children—male and female—of *all* such parents as were not owners of real estate of the yearly value of $500, had been—no matter how long—held in slavery by their more wealthy landholding neighbors ;—would Congress, under the Constitution, have a right (by recognising) to establish, for ever, such a relation as one white person, under such a law, might hold to another? Surely not. And yet no substantial difference between the two cases can be pointed out.

* Mr. Clay, in conducting the Missouri compromise, found it necessary to argue, that the admission of Missouri, as a slaveholding state, would *aid* in bringing about the termination of slavery. His argument is thus stated by Mr. Sergeant, who replied to him :—" In this long view of remote and distant consequences, the gentleman from Kentucky (Mr. Clay) thinks he sees how slavery,

succeeded in blinding the confiding people of the North. They thought for the most part, that the slaveholders were acting in good faith. It is not intended by this remark, to make the impression, that the South had all along pressed the admission of new slave states, simply with a view to the increase of its own relative power. By no means : slavery had insinuated itself into favor because of its being mixed up with (other) supposed benefits—and because its ultimate influence on the government was neither suspected nor dreaded. But, on the Missouri question, there was a fair trial of strength between the friends of Slavery and the friends of the Constitution. The former triumphed, and by the prime agency of one whose raiment, the remainder of his days, ought to be sackcloth and ashes,—because of the disgrace he has continued on the name of his country, and the consequent injury that he has inflicted on the cause of Freedom throughout the world. Although all the different Administrations, from the first organization of the government, had, in the indirect manner already mentioned, favored slavery,—there had not been on any previous occasion, a direct struggle between its pretensions and the principles of liberty ingrafted on the Constitution. The friends of the latter were induced to believe, whenever they should be arrayed against each other, that *theirs* would be the triumph. Tremendous error! Mistake almost fatal! The battle was fought. Slavery emerged from it unhurt—her hands made gory—her bloody plume still floating in the air—exultingly brandishing her dripping sword over her prostrate and vanquished enemy. She had won all for which she fought. Her victory was complete—THE SANCTION OF THE NATION WAS GIVEN TO SLAVERY!*

Immediately after this achievement, the slaveholding interest was still more strongly fortified by the acquisition of Florida, and the establishment of slavery there, as it had already been in the territory of Louisiana. The Missouri triumph, however, seems to have extinguished every thing like a systematic or spirited opposition, on the part of the free states, to the pretensions of the slaveholding South.

Arkansas was admitted but the other day, with nothing that deserves to be called an effort to prevent it—although her Constitution attempts

---

when thus spread, is at last to find its end. It is to be brought about by the combined operation of the laws which regulate the price of labor, and the laws which govern population. When the country shall be filled with inhabitants, and the price of labor shall have reached a minimum, (a comparative minimum I suppose is meant,) free labor will be found cheaper than slave labor. Slaves will then be without employment, and, of course, without the means of comfortable subsistence, which will reduce their numbers, and finally extirpate them. This is the argument as I understand it," says Mr. Sergeant ; and, certainly, one more chimerical or more inhuman could not have been urged.

    * See Appendix, E.

to *perpetuate* slavery, by forbidding the master to emancipate his bondmen without the consent of the Legislature, and the Legislature without the consent of the master.   Emboldened, but not satisfied, with their success in every political contest with the people of the free states, the slaveholders are begining now to throw off their disguise—to brand their former notions about the " *evil*, political and moral" of slavery, as " folly and delusion,"*—and as if to " make assurance double sure," and defend themselves forever, by territoral power, against the progress of Free

* Mr. Calhoun is reported, in the National Intelligencer, as having used these words in a speech delivered in the Senate, the 10th day of January :—

" Many in the South once believed that it [slavery] was a moral and political evil ; that folly and delusion are gone. We see it now in its true light, and regard it as the most safe and stable basis for free institutions in the world."

Mr. Hammond, formerly a Representative in Congress from South Carolina, delivered a speech (Feb. 1, 1836) on the question of receiving petitions for the abolition of slavery in the District of Columbia. In answering those who objected to a slaveholding country, that it was " assimilated to an aristocracy," he says—" In this they are right. I accept the terms. *It is a government of the best*. Combining all the advantages, and possessing but few of the disadvantages, of the aristocracy of the old world—without fostering, to an unwarrantable extent, the pride, the exclusiveness, the selfishness, the thirst for sway, the contempt for the rights of others, which distinguish the nobility of Europe—it gives us their education, their polish, their munificence, their high honor, their undaunted spirit. Slavery does indeed create an aristocracy—an aristocracy of talents, of virtue, of generosity, of courage. In a slave country, every freeman is an aristocrat. Be he rich or poor, if he does not possess a single slave, he has been born to all the natural advantages of the society in which he is placed ; and all its honors lie open before him, inviting his genius and industry. Sir, I do firmly believe, that domestic slavery, regulated as ours is, produces the highest toned, the purest, best organization of society, that has ever existed on the face of the earth."

That this *retraxit* of former *follies and delusions* is not confined to the mere politician, we have the following proofs :—

The CHARLESTON (S. C.) UNION PRESBYTERY—" Resolved, That in the opinion of this Presbytery, the holding of slaves, so far from being a SIN in the sight of God, is nowhere condemned in his holy word ; that it is in accordance with the example, or consistent with the precepts, of patriarchs, prophets, and apostles ; and that it is compatible with the most fraternal regard to the good of the servants whom God has committed to our charge."—Within the last few months, as we learn from a late No. of the Charleston Courier, the late Synod of the Presbyterian Church, in Augusta, (Ga.) passed resolutions declaring " That slavery is a CIVIL INSTITUTION, with which the General Assembly [the highest ecclesiastical tribunal] has NOTHING TO DO."

Again :—The CHARLESTON BAPTIST ASSOCIATION, in a memorial to the Legislature of South Carolina, say—" The undersigned would further represent, that the said Association does not consider that the Holy Scriptures have made the FACT of slavery a question of morals at all." And further,—" The right of masters to dispose of the time of their slaves, has been distinctly recognised by the Creator of all things."

Again :—The EDGEFIELD (S. C.) ASSOCIATION—" Resolved, That the practical question of slavery, in a country where the system has obtained as a part of its stated policy, is settled in the Scriptures by Jesus Christ and his apostles." " Resolved, That these uniformly recognised the relation of master and slave, and enjoined on both their respective duties, under a system of servitude more degrading and absolute than that which obtains in our country."

Again we find, in a late No. of the Charleston Courier, the following :—

" THE SOUTHERN CHURCH.—The Georgia Conference of the Methodist Episcopal Church, at a recent meeting in Athens, passed resolutions, declaring that slavery, as it exists in the United States, is not a moral evil, and is a civil and domestic institution, with which Christian ministers have nothing to do, further than to meliorate the condition of the slave, by endeavoring to impart to him and his master the benign influence of the religion of Christ, and aiding both on their way to heaven."

5

principles and the renovation of the Constitution, they now demand openly—scorning to conceal that their object is, to *advance and establish their political power in the country,*—that Texas, a foreign state, five or six times as large as all New England, with a Constitution dyed as deep in slavery as that of Arkansas, shall be added to the Union.

The abolitionists feel a deep regard for the integrity and union of the government, *on the principles of the Constitution.* Therefore it is, that they look with earnest concern on the attempt now making by the South, to do, what, in the view of multitudes of our citizens, would amount to good cause for the separation of the free from the slave states. Their concern is not mingled with any feelings of despair. The alarm they sounded on the "annexation" question has penetrated the free states; it will, in all probability, be favorably responded to by every one of them; thus giving encouragement to our faith, that the admission of Texas will be successfully resisted.—that this additional stain will not be impressed on our national escutcheon. nor this additional peril brought upon the South.*

This, the present condition of the country, induced by a long train of usurpations on the part of the South, and by unworthy concessions to it by the North, may justly be regarded as one of the events of the last few years affecting in some way, the measures of the abolitionists It has certainly done so. And whilst it is not to be denied, that many abolitionists feel painful apprehensions for the result, it has only roused them up to make more strenuous efforts for the preservation of the country.

It may be replied—if the abolitionists are such firm friends of the Union, why do they persist in what must end in its rupture and dissolution ? The abolitionists, let it be repeated *are* friends of *the* Union that was intended by the Constitution; but not of a Union from which is eviscerated, to be trodden under foot, the right to SPEAK,—to PRINT —to PETITION,—the rights of CONSCIENCE; not of a Union whose lig aments are whips, where the interest of the oppressor is the *great* interest, the right to oppress the *paramount* right. It is against the distortion of the glorious Union our fathers left us into one bound with despotic bands that the abolitionists are contending. In the political aspect of the question, they have nothing to ask, except what the Constitution authorizes—no change to desire, but that the Constitution may be restored to its pristine republican purity.

But they have well considered the "dissolution of the Union.'

* See Appendix, F.

There is no just ground for apprehending that such a measure will
ever be resorted to by the *South*. It is by no means intended by this,
to affirm, that the South, like a spoiled child, for the first time denied
some favourite object, may not fall into sudden frenzy and do herself
some great harm. But knowing as I do, the intelligence and forecast of
the leading men of the South—and believing that they will, if ever such
a crisis should come, be judiciously influenced by the *existing* state of
the case, and by the *consequences* that would inevitably flow from an
act of dissolution—they would not, I am sure, deem it desirable or
politic. They would be brought, in their calmer moments, to coincide
with one who has facetiously, but not the less truly remarked, that it
would be as indiscreet in the slave South to separate from the free
North, as for the poor, to separate from the parish that supported them.
In support of this opinion, I would say :

First—A dissolution of the Union by the South would, in no manner, secure to her the object she has in view.—The *leaders* at the
South, both in the church and in the state, must, by this time, be too
well informed as to the nature of the anti-slavery movement, and the
character of those engaged in it, to entertain fears that, violence of any
kind will be resorted to, directly or indirectly.* The whole complaint
of the South is neither more nor less than this—THE NORTH TALKS
ABOUT SLAVERY. Now, of all the means or appliances that could be
devised, to give greater life and publicity to the discussion of slavery,
none could be half so effectual as the dissolution of the Union *because
of the discussion*. It would astonish the civilized world—they would
inquire into the cause of such a remarkable event in its history ;—the
result would be not only enlarged *discussion* of the whole subject,
but it would bring such a measure of contempt on the guilty movers of
the deed, that even with all the advantages of " their education, their
polish, their munificence, their high honor, their undaunted spirit," so
eloquently set forth by the Hon. Mr. Hammond, they would find it hard
to withstand its influence. It is difficult for men in a *good* cause, to
maintain their steadfastness in opposition to an extensively corrupt
public sentiment ; in a *bad* one, against public sentiment purified and
enlightened, next to impossible, if not quite so.

Another result would follow the dissolution :—*Now*, the abolitionists

---

* " It is not," says Mr. Calhoun, " that we expect the abolitionists will resort to arms—will
commence a crusade to deliver our slaves by force."—" Let me tell our friends of the South, who
differ from us, that the war which the abolitionists wage against us is of a very different character, and *far more effective*. It is waged, not against our lives, but our character." More correctly,
Mr. C. might have said against a *system*, with which the slaveholders have chosen to involve their
characters, and which they have determined to defend, at the hazard of losing them

find it difficult, by reason of the odium which the principal slaveholders and their friends have succeeded in attaching to their *name*, to introduce a knowledge of their principles and measures into the great mass of southern mind. There are multitudes at the South who would co-operate with us, if they could be informed of our aim.* Now, we cannot reach them— then, it would be otherwise. The united power of the large slaveholders would not be able longer to keep them in ignorance. If the Union were dissolved, they *would* know the cause, and discuss it, and condemn it.

A second reason why the South will not dissolve the Union is, that she would be exposed to the visitation of *real* incendiaries, exciting her slaves to revolt. Now, it would cover any one with infamy, who would stir them up to vindicate their rights by the massacre of their masters. Dissolve the Union, and the candidates for "GLORY" would find in the plains of Carolina and Louisiana as inviting a theatre for their enterprise, as their prototypes, the Houstons, the Van Rennsselaers, and the Sutherlands did, in the prairies of Texas or the forests of Canada.

A third reason why the South will not dissolve is, that the slaves would leave their masters and take refuge in the free states. The South would not be able to establish a *cordon* along her wide frontier sufficiently strong to prevent it. Then, the slaves could not be reclaimed, as they now are, under the Constitution. Some may say, the free states would not permit them to come in and dwell among them.—Believe it not. The fact of separation on the ground supposed, would abolitionize the whole North. Beside this, in an economical point of view, the *demand for labor* in the Western States would make their presence welcome. At all events, a passage through the Northern States to Canada would not be denied them.

A fourth reason why the South will not dissolve is, that a large number of her most steady and effective population would emigrate to the free states. In the slave-*selling* states especially, there has always been a class who have consented to remain there with their families, only in the hope that slavery would, in some way or other, be termina-

---

* There is abundant evidence of this. Our limits confine us to the following, from the first No. of the Southern Literary Journal, (Charleston, S. C.) :—" There are *many good men even among us*, who have began to grow *timid*. They think, that what the virtuous and high-minded men of the North look upon as a crime and a plague-spot, cannot be perfectly innocent or quite harmless in a slaveholding community '

This, also, from the North Carolina Watchman :—

" It (the abolition party) is the growing party at the North. We are inclined to believe that there is even more of it at the South than prudence will permit to be openly avowed."

" It is well known, Mr. Speaker, that there is a LARGE, RESPECTABLE and INTELLIGENT PARTY in Kentucky, who will exert every nerve and spare no efforts to dislodge the subsisting rights to our slave population, or alter in some manner, and to some extent, at least, the tenure by which that species of property is held."—*Speech of the Hon. James T. Morehead in the Kentucky Legislature, last winter.*

ted. I do not say they are abolitionists, for many of them are slave-holders. It may be, too, that such would expect compensation for their slaves, should they be emancipated, and also that they should be sent out of the country. The particular mode of emancipation, however crude it may be, that has occupied their minds, has nothing to do with the point before us. *They look for emancipation—in this hope they have remained, and now remain, where they are.* Take away this hope, by making slavery the *distinctive bond of union* of a new government, and you drive them to the North. These persons are not among the rich, the voluptuous, the effeminate; nor are they the despised, the indigent, the thriftless—they are men of moderate property, of intelligence, of conscience—in every way the "bone and sinew" of the South.

A fifth reason why the South will not dissolve, is her *weakness.* It is a remarkable fact, that in modern times, and in the Christian world, all slaveholding countries have been united with countries that are free. Thus, the West Indian and Mexican and South American slaveholding colonies were united to England, France, Spain, Portugal, and other states of Europe. If England (before her Emancipation Act) and the others had at any time withdrawn the protection of their *power* from their colonies, slavery would have been extinguished almost simultane-ously with the knowledge of the fact. In the West Indies there could have been no doubt of this, from the disparity in numbers between the whites and the slaves, from the multiplied attempts made from time to time by the latter to vindicate their rights by insurrection, and from the fact, that all their insurrections had to be suppressed by the *force* of the mother country. As soon as Mexico and the South American colonies dissolved their connexion with Spain, slavery was abolished in every one of them. This may, I know, be attributed to the neces-sity imposed on these states, by the wars in which they engaged to establish their independence. However this may be—the *fact* still remains. The free states of this Union are to the slave, so far as the maintenance of slavery is concerned, substantially, in the relation of the European states to their slaveholding colonies. Slavery, in all pro-bability, could not be maintained by the South disjoined from the North, a single year. So far from there existing any reason for making the South an exception, in this particular, to other slave countries, there are circumstances in her condition that seem to make her depen-dence more complete. Two of them are, the superior intelligence of her slaves on the subject of human rights, and the geographical con-nexion of the slave region in the United States. In the West Indies, in Mexico and South America the great body of the slaves were far below the slaves of this country in their intellectual and moral condition—and their power to act in concert was weakened by the insular fragments into which they were divided.

Again, the depopulation of the South of large numbers of its white inhabitants, from the cause mentioned under the fourth head, would, it is apprehended, bring the two classes to something like a numerical equality. Now, consider the present state of the moral sentiment of the Christianized and commercial world in relation to slavery; add to it the impulse that this sentiment, acknowledged by the South already to be wholly opposed to her, would naturally acquire by an act of separation on her part, with a single view to the perpetuation of slavery; bring this sentiment in all its accumulation and intensity to act upon a nation where one half are enslavers, the other the enslaved—and what must be the effect? From the nature of mind; from the laws of moral influence, (which are as sure in their operation, if not so well understood, as the laws of physical influence,) the party " whose conscience with injustice is oppressed," must become dispirited, weakened in courage, and in the end unnerved and contemptible. On the other hand, the sympathy that would be felt for the oppressed—the comfort they would receive—the encouragement that would be given them to assert their rights, would make it an impossibility, to keep them in slavish peace and submission.

This state of things would be greatly aggravated by the peculiarly morbid sensitiveness of the South to every thing that is supposed to touch her *character*. Her highest distinction would then become her most troublesome one. How, for instance, could her chivalrous sons bear to be taunted, wherever they went, on business or for pleasure, out of their own limits, with the cry " the knights of the lash !" " Go home and pay your laborers !" " Cease from the scourging of husbands and wives in each others presence—from attending the shambles, to sell or buy as slaves those whom God has made of the same blood with yourselves—your brethren—your sisters ! Cease, high minded sons of the ' ANCIENT DOMINION,' from estimating your revenue by the number of children you rear, to sell in the flesh market !" " Go home and pay your laborers !" " Go home and pay your laborers !" This would be a trial to which " southern chivalry" could not patiently submit. Their " high honor," their " undaunted spirit" would impel them to the field—only to prove that the " last resort" requires something more substantial than mere " honor" and " spirit" to maintain it. Suppose there should be a disagreement—as in all likelihood there soon would, leading to war between the North and the South ? The

North would scarcely have occasion to march a squadron to the field. She would have an army that could be raised up by the million, at the fireside of her enemy. It has been said, that during the late war with England, it was proposed to her cabinet, by some enterprising officers, to land five thousand men on the coast of South Carolina and proclaim liberty to the slaves. The success of the scheme was well thought of. But then the example! England herself held nearly a million of slaves at no greater distance from the scene of action than the West Indies. *Now*, a restraint of this kind on such a scheme does not exist.

It seems plain beyond the power of argument to make it plainer, that a slaveholding nation—one under the circumstances in which the South separated from the North would be placed—must be at the mercy of every free people having neither power to vindicate a right nor avenge a wrong.*

A sixth reason why the South will not dissolve the Union, is found in the difficulty of bringing about an *actual* separation. Preparatory to such a movement, it would seem indispensable, that *Union* among the seceding states themselves should be secured. A General Convention would be necessary to adjust its terms. This would, of course, be preceded by *particular* conventions in the several states. To this procedure the same objection applies, that has been made, for the last two or three years, to holding an anti-abolition convention in the South :— It would give to the *question* such notoriety, that the object of holding the convention could not be concealed from the slaves. The more sagacious in the South have been opposed to a convention ; nor have they been influenced solely by the consideration just mentioned— which, in my view, is but of little moment—but by the apprehension, that the diversity of sentiment which exists among the slave states, themselves, in relation to the *system*, would be disclosed to the country ; and that the slaveholding interest would be found deficient in that harmony which, from its perfectness heretofore, has made the slaveholders so successful in their action on the North.

The slaveholding region may be divided into the *farming* and the *planting*—or the slave-*selling* and the slave-*buying* districts. Maryland, Virginia, Kentucky, Missouri and East Tennessee constitute the first.

* Governor Hayne, of South Carolina, spoke in high terms, a few years ago, of the ability that the South would possess, in a military point of view, because her great wealth would enable her, at all times, to command the services of mercenary troops. Without stopping to dispute with him. as to her comparative wealth, I would remark, that he seemed entirely to have overlooked this truth—that whenever a government is under the necessity of calling in foreign troops, to keep in subjection one half of the people, the *power* of the government has already passed into the hands of the *Protectors*. They can and will, of course, act with whichever party will best subserve their purpose.

West Tennessee is somewhat equivocal. All the states south of Tennessee belong to the slave-*buying* district. The first, with but few exceptions, have from the earliest times, felt slavery a reproach to their good name—an encumbrance on their advancement—at some period, to be cast off. This sentiment, had it been at all encouraged by the action of the General Government, in accordance with the views of the convention that formed the Constitution, would, in all probability, by this time, have brought slavery in Maryland and Virginia to an end. Notwithstanding the easy admission of slave states into the Union, and the *yielding* of the free states whenever they were brought in collision with the South, have had a strong tendency to persuade the *farming* slave states to continue their system, yet the sentiment in favor of emancipation in some form, still exists among them. Proof, encouraging proof of this, is found in the present attitude of Kentucky. Her legislature has just passed a law, proposing to the people, to hold a convention to alter the constitution. In the discussion of the bill, slavery as connected with some form of emancipation, seems to have constituted the most important element. The public journals too, that are *opposed* to touching the subject at all, declare that the main object for recommending a a convention was, to act on slavery in some way.

Now, it would be in vain for the *planting* South to expect, that Kentucky or any other of the *farming* slave states would unite with her, in making slavery the *perpetual bond* of a new political organization. If they feel the inconveniences of slavery *in their present condition*, they could not be expected to enter on another, where these inconveniences would be inconceivably multiplied and aggravated, and, by the very terms of their new contract, *perpetuated*.

This letter is already so protracted, that I cannot stop here to develop more at large this part of the subject. To one acquainted with the state of public sentiment, in what I have called, the *farming* district, it needs no further development. There is not one of these states embraced in it, that would not, when brought to the test, prefer the privileges of the Union to the privilege of perpetual slaveholding. And if there should turn out to be a single *desertion* in this matter, the whole project of secession must come to nought.

But laying aside all the obstacles to union among the seceding states, how is it possible to take the first step to *actual* separation! The separation, at the worst, can only be *political*. There will be no chasm—no rent made in the earth between the two sections. The natural and ideal boundaries will remain unaltered. Mason and Dixon's line will not become a wall of adamant that can neither be undermined nor surmounted. The Ohio river will not be converted into flame, or into another Styx, denying a passage to every living thing,

Besides this stability of natural things, the multiform interests of the two sections would, in the main, continue as they are. The complicate ties of commerce could not be suddenly unloosed. The bread-stuffs, the beef, the pork, the turkies, the chickens, the woollen and cotton fabrics, the hats, the shoes, the socks, the " *horn flints and bark nutmegs,*"* the machinery, the sugar-kettles, the cotton-gins, the axes, the hoes, the drawing-chains of the North, would be as much needed by the South, the day after the separation as the day before. The newspapers of the North—its Magazines, its Quarterlies, its Monthlies, would be more sought after by the readers of the South than they now are ; and the Southern journals would become doubly interesting to us. There would be the same lust for our northern summers and your southern winters, with all their health-giving influences ; and last, though not least, the same desire of marrying and of being given in marriage that now exists between the North and South. Really it is difficult to say *where* this long threatened separation is to *begin ;* and if the place of beginning could be found, it would seem like a poor exchange for the South, to give up all these pleasant and profitable relations and connections for the privilege of enslaving an equal number of their fellow-creatures.

Thus much for the menace, that the " UNION WILL BE DISSOLVED" unless the discussion of the slavery question be stopped.

But you may reply, " Do you think the South is not in earnest in her threat of dissolving the Union ?" I rejoin, by no means ;—yet she pursues a perfectly reasonable course (leaving out of view the justice or morality of it)—just such a course as I should expect she would pursue, emboldened as she must be by her multiplied triumphs over the North by the use of the same weapon. " We'll dissolve the Union !" was the cry, " unless Missouri be admitted ! !" The North were frightened, and Missouri was admitted with SLAVERY engraved on her forehead. " We'll dissolve the Union !" unless the Indians be driven out of the South ! ! The North forgot her treaties, parted with humanity, and it is done—the defenceless Indians are forced to " consent" to be driven out, or they are left, undefended, to the mercies of southern land-jobbers and gold-hunters. " We'll dissolve the Union ! If the Tariff" [established at her own suggestion] " be not repealed or modified so that our slave-labor may compete with your free-labor."

* Senator Preston's Railroad Speech, delivered at Columbia, S. C., in 1836.

6

The Tariff is accordingly modified to suit the South. " We'll dissolve the Union!" unless the freedom of speech and the press be put down in the North!!—With the promptness of commission-merchants, the alternative is adopted. Public assemblies met for deliberation are assailed and broken up at the North ; her citizens are stoned and beaten and dragged through the streets of her cities ; her presses are attacked by mobs, instigated and led on by men of influence and character ; whilst those concerned in conducting them are compelled to fly from their homes, pursued as if they were noxious wild beasts ; or, if they remain to defend, they are sacrificed to appease the southern divinity. " We'll dissolve the Union" if slavery be abolished in the District of of Columbia ! The North, frightened from her propriety, declares that slavery ought not to be abolished there NOW.—" We'll dissolve the Union !" if you read petitions from your constituents for its abolition, or for stopping the slave-trade at the Capital, or between the states. FIFTY NORTHERN REPRESENTATIVES respond to the cry, " down, then, with the RIGHT OF PETITION !!" All these assaults have succeeded because the North has been frightened by the war-cry, " WE'LL DISSOLVE THE UNION !"

After achieving so much by a process so simple, why should not the South persist in it when striving for further conquests ? No other course ought to be expected from her, till this has failed. And it is not at all improbable, that she will persist, till she almost persuades herself that she is serious in her menace to dissolve the Union. She may in her eagerness, even approach so near the verge of dissolution, that the earth may give way under her feet and she be dashed in ruins in the gulf below.

Nothing will more surely arrest her fury, than the firm array of the North, setting up anew the almost forgotten principles of our fathers, and saying to the " dark spirit of slavery,"—" thus far shalt thou go, and no farther." This is the best—the only—means of saving the South from the fruits of her own folly—folly that has been so long, and so strangely encouraged by the North, that it has grown into intolerable arrogance—down right presumption.

There are many other " events" of the last two or three years which have, doubtless, had their influence on the course of the abolitionists— and which might properly be dwelt upon at considerable length, were it not that this communication is already greatly protracted beyond its intended limits. I shall, therefore, in mentioning the remaining topics, do little more than enumerate them.

The Legislature of Vermont has taken a decided stand in favor of anti-slavery principles and action. In the Autumn of 1836, the following resolutions were passed by an almost unanimous vote in both houses :—

" Resolved, By the General Assembly of the State of Vermont, That neither Congress nor the State Governments have any constitutional right to abridge the free expressions of opinions, or the transmission of them through the medium of the public mails."

" Resolved, That Congress do possess the power to abolish slavery in the District of Columbia."

" Resolved, That His Excellency, the Governor, be requested to transmit a copy of the foregoing resolutions to the Executive of each of the States, and to each of our Senators and Representatives in Congress."

At the session held in November last, the following joint resolutions, preceded by a decisive memorial against the admission of Texas, were passed by both branches—with the exception of the *fifth*, which was passed only by the House of Representatives :—

1. Resolved, By the Senate and House of Representatives, That our Senators in Congress be instructed, and our Representatives requested, to use their influence in that body to prevent the annexation of Texas to the Union.

2. Resolved, That, representing, as we do, the people of Vermont, we do hereby, in their name, SOLEMNLY PROTEST against such annexation in any form.

3. Resolved, That, as the Representatives of the people of Vermont, we do solemnly protest against the admission, into this Union, of any state whose constitution tolerates domestic slavery.

4. Resolved, That Congress have full power, by the Constitution, to abolish slavery and the slave-trade in the District of Columbia and in the territories of the United States.

[5. Resolved, That Congress has the constitutional power to prohibit the slave-trade between the several states of this Union, and to make such laws as shall effectually prohibit such trade.]

6. Resolved, That our Senators in Congress be instructed, and our Representatives requested, to present the foregoing Report and Resolutions to their respective Houses in Congress, and use their influence to carry the same speedily into effect.

7. Resolved, That the Governor of this State be requested to transmit a copy of the foregoing Report and Resolutions to the President of the United States, and to each of our Senators and Representatives in Congress.

The influence of anti-slavery principles in Massachusetts has become decisive, if we are to judge from the change of sentiment in the legislative body. The governor of that commonwealth saw fit to introduce into his inaugural speech, delivered in January, 1836, a severe censure of the abolitionists, and to intimate that they were guilty of an offence punishable at common law. This part of the speech was referred to a joint committee of five, of which a member of the senate was chairman. To the same committee were also referred communications which had been received by the governor from several of the legislatures of the slaveholding states, requesting the Legislature of Massachusetts to enact laws, making it PENAL for citizens of that state to form societies for the abolition of slavery, or to speak or publish sentiments such as had been uttered in anti-slavery meetings and published in anti-slavery tracts and papers. The managers of the Massachusetts Anti-Slavery Society, in a note addressed to the chairman of the committee, requested permission, as a party whose rights were drawn in question, to appear before it. This was granted. The gentlemen selected by them to appear on their behalf were of unimpeachable character, and distinguished for professional merit and general literary and scientific intelligence. Such was *then* the unpopularity of abolitionism, that notwithstanding the personal influence of these gentlemen, they were ill—not to say rudely—treated, especially by the chairman of the committee ; so much so, that respect for themselves, and the cause they were deputed to defend, persuaded them to desist before they had completed their remarks. A Report, including Resolutions unfavorable to the abolitionists was made, of which the following is a copy :—

The Joint Special Committee, to whom was referred so much of the governor's message as related to the abolition of slavery, together with certain documents upon the same subject, communicated to the Executive by the several Legislatures of Virginia, North Carolina, South Carolina, Georgia, and Alabama, transmitted by his Excellency to the Legislature, and hereunto annexed, have considered the same, and ask leave, respectfully, to submit the following :—

Resolved, That this Legislature distinctly disavow any right whatever in itself, or in the citizens of this commonwealth, to interfere in the institution of domestic slavery in the southern states : it having existed therein before the establishment of the Constitution ; it having been recognised by that instrument ; and it being strictly within their own keeping.

Resolved, That this Legislature, regarding the agitation of the question of domestic slavery as having already interrupted the friendly relations which ought to exist between the several states of this Union, and as tending permanently to injure, if not altogether to subvert, the principles of the Union itself ; and believing that the good effected by those who excite its discussion in the non-slaveholding states is, under the circumstances of the case, altogether visionary, while the immediate and future evil is great and certain ; does hereby express its entire disapprobation of the doctrine upon this subject avowed, and the general measures pursued by such as agitate the question ; and does earnestly recommend to them carefully to abstain from all such discussion, and all such measures, as may tend to disturb and irritate the public mind.

The report was laid on the table, whence it was not taken up during the session—its friends being afraid of a lean majority on its passage ; for the *alarm* had already been taken by many of the members who otherwise would have favored it. From this time till the election in the succeeding autumn, the subject was much agitated in Massachusetts. The abolitionists again petitioned the Legislature at its session begun in January, 1837; especially, that it should remonstrate against the resolution of Mr. Hawes, adopted by the House of Representatives in Congress, by which all memorials, &c, in relation to slavery were laid, and to be laid, on the table, without further action on them. The abolitionists were again heard, in behalf of their petitions, before the proper committee.* The result was, the passage of the following resolutions with only 16 dissenting voices to 378, in the House of Representatives, and in the Senate with not more than one or two dissentients on any one of them :—

"Whereas, The House of Representatives of the United States, in the month of January, in the year of our Lord one thousand eight hundred and thirty-seven, did adopt a resolution, whereby it was ordered that all petitions, memorials, resolutions, propositions, or papers, relating in any way, or to any extent whatever, to the subject of slavery, or the abolition of slavery, without being either printed or referred, should be laid upon the table, and that no further action whatever should be had thereon ; and whereas such a disposition of petitions, then or thereafter to be received, is a virtual denial of the right itself; and whereas, by the resolution aforesaid, which is adopted as a standing rule in the present House of Representatives, the petitions of a large number of the people of this commonwealth, praying for the removal of a great social, moral, and political evil, have been slighted and contemned : therefore,—

"Resolved, That the resolution above named is an assumption of power and authority at variance with the spirit and intent of the Constitution of the United States, and injurious to the cause of freedom and free institutions ; that it does violence to the inherent, absolute, and inalienable rights of man ; and that it tends, essentially, to impair those fundamental principles of natural justice and natural law which are antecedent to any written constitutions of government, independent of them all, and essential to the security of freedom in a state.

"Resolved, That our Senators and Representatives in Congress, in maintaining and advocating the right of petition, have entitled themselves to the cordial approbation of the people of this commonwealth.

"Resolved, That Congress, having exclusive legislation in the District of Columbia, possess the right to abolish slavery in said district, and that its exercise should only be restrained by a regard to the public good."

That you may judge, what yourself, influence the abolition question exercised in the elections in Massachusetts *last* autumn, I send you three numbers of the Liberator containing copies of letters addressed to many of the candidates, and their respective answers.

The Legislature have passed, *unanimously*, at its present session, resolutions (preceded by a report of great ability) protesting " *earnestly*

---

* The gentleman who had been chairman of the committee the preceding year, was supposed, in consequence of the change in public opinion in relation to abolitionists, to have injured his political standing too much, even to be nominated as a candidate for re-election.

and solemnly against the annexation of Texas to this Union;" and declaring that, *"no act done, or compact made, for such purpose, by the government of the United States, will be binding on the states or the people."*

Two years ago, Governor Marcy, of this state, showed himself willing, at the dictation of the South, to aid in passing laws for restraining and punishing the abolitionists, whenever the extremity of the case might call for it. Two weeks ago, at the request of the Young Men's Anti-Slavery Society of Albany, the Assembly-chamber, by a vote of the House (only two dissentient) was granted to Alvan Stewart, Esq., a distinguished lawyer, to lecture on the subject of abolition.

Kentucky is assuming an attitude of great interest to the friends of Liberty and the Constitution. The blessings of " them that are ready to perish" throughout the land, the applause of the good throughout the world will be hers, if she should show moral energy enough to break every yoke that she has hitherto imposed on the " poor," and by which her own prosperity and true power have been hindered.

In view of the late action in the Senate and House of Representatives in Congress—adverse as they may seem, to those who think more highly of the branches of the Legislature than of the SOURCE of their power—the abolitionists see nothing that is cause for discouragement. They find the PEOPLE sound ; they know that they still cherish, as their fathers did, the right of petition—the freedom of the press—the freedom of speech—the rights of conscience ; that they love the liberty of the North more than they love the slavery of the South. What care they for *Resolutions* in the House, or Resolutions in the Senate, when the House and the Senate are but their ministers, their servants, and they know that they can discharge them at their pleasure ? It may be, that Congress has yet to learn, that the people have but slight regard for their restraining resolutions. They ought to have known this from the history of such resolutions for the last two years. THIRTY-SEVEN THOUSAND petitioners for the abolition of slavery in the District of Columbia had their petitions laid on the table by the resolution of the House of Representatives in May, 1836. At the succeeding session, they had increased to ONE HUNDRED AND TEN THOUSAND.—The resolution of Jan. 18, 1837, laid all *their* petitions in the same way on the table. At the *called*, and at the present session, these 110,000 had multiplied to FIVE HUNDRED THOUSAND.* *Soon*, Senators and Representatives will be sent from the free states who will need no petitions —they will know the prayer of their constituents *before they leave their homes.*

* See Appendix, G.

In concluding this, my answer to your 13th interrogatory, I will say that I know of no event, that has transpired, either in or out of Congress, for the last two or three years, that has had any other influence on the efforts of abolitionists than to increase and stimulate them. Indeed, every thing that has taken place within that period, ought to excite to their utmost efforts all who are not despairing dastards. The Demon of oppression in this land is tenfold more fierce and rampant and relentless than he was supposed to be before roused from the quiet of his lair. To every thing that is precious the abolitionists have seen him lay claim. The religion of the Bible must be adulterated—the claims of Humanity must be smothered—the demands of justice must be nullified—a part of our Race must be shut out from the common sympathy of a common nature. Nor is this all: they see their *own* rights and those of the people; the right to SPEAK—to WRITE—to PRINT—to PUBLISH—to ASSEMBLE TOGETHER—to PETITION THEIR OWN SERVANTS—all brought in peril. They feel that the final conflict between Popular liberty and Aristocratic slavery has come; that one or the other must fall; and they have made up their minds, with the blessing of God on their efforts, that their adversary shall die.

" 14. *Have you any permanent fund, and how much?*

ANSWER.—We have none. The contributions are anticipated. We are always in debt, and always getting out of debt.

I have now, Sir, completed my answers to the questions proposed in your letter of the 16th ult. It gives me pleasure to have had such an auspicious opportunity of doing so. I cannot but hope for good to both the parties concerned, where candor and civility have characterized their representatives.

Part of the answer to your 13th question may seem to wander from the strict terms of the question proposed. Let it be set down to a desire, on my part, to give you all the information I can, at all germain to the inquiry. The " proffer," made in my note to Mr. Calhoun, was not " unguarded ;"—nor was it *singular*. The information I have furnished has been always accessible to our adversaries—even though the application for it might not have been clothed in the polite and gentlemanly terms which have so strongly recommended yours to the most respectful consideration of

Your very obedient servant,

JAMES G. BIRNEY.

[In the Explanatory Remarks placed at the beginning of this Correspondence, reasons were given, that were deemed sufficient, for not publishing more of the letters that passed between Mr. Elmore and myself than the two above. Since they were in type, I have received from Mr. Elmore a communication, in reply to one from me, informing him that I proposed limiting the publication to the two letters just mentioned. It is dated May 19. The following extract shows that he entertains a different opinion from mine, and thinks that justice to him requires that *another* of his letters should be included in the Correspondence :—

" The order you propose in the publication is proper enough ; the omission of business and immaterial letters being perfectly proper, as they can interest nobody. I had supposed my last letter would have formed an exception to the rule, which excluded immaterial papers. It explained, more fully than my first, my reasons for this correspondence, defined the limits to *which I had prescribed myself*, and was a proper accompaniment to *a publication* of what *I* had not written for publication. Allow me, Sir, to say, that it will be but bare justice to me that it should be printed with the other papers. I only suggest this for your own consideration, for—adhering to my former opinions and decision—I ask nothing and complain of nothing."

It is still thought that the publication of the letter alluded to is unnecessary to the purpose of enlightening the public, as to the state, prospects, &c, of the anti-slavery cause. It contains no denial of the facts, nor impeachment of the statements, nor answer to the arguments, presented in my communication. But as Mr. Elmore is personally interested in this matter, and as it is intended to maintain the consistent liberality which has characterized the Executive Committee in all their intercourse with their opponents, the suggestion made by Mr. Elmore is cheerfully complied with. The following is a copy of the letter alluded to.—J. G. B.]

"WASHINGTON, May 5, 1838.
" To JAMES G. BIRNEY, Esq., Cor. Sec. A. A. S. S.

" SIR,—I have to acknowledge the receipt of your letter of the 1st instant, in which you again refer to the publication of the Correspondence between us, in relation to the measures and designs of the abolitionists. I would have certainly answered yours of the 2d ult., on the same subject, more fully before this, had it not escaped my recollection, in consequence [of] having been more engaged than usual in the business before the House. I hope the delay has been productive of no inconvenience.

" If I correctly understand your letters above referred to, the control of these papers, and the decision as to their publication, have passed into the ' Executive Committee of the American Anti-Slavery Society ;'

and, from their tenor, I infer that their determination is so far made, that nothing I could object would prevent it, if I desired to do so. I was certainly not apprised, when I entered into this Correspondence, that its disposition was to depend on any other will than yours and mine,—but that matters nothing now,—you had the power, and I am not disposed to question the right or propriety of its exercise. I heard of you as a man of intelligence, sincerity, and truth,—who, although laboring in a bad cause, did it with ability, and from a mistaken conviction of its justice. As one of the Representatives of a slave-holding constituency, and one of a committee raised by the Representatives of the slave-holding States, to ascertain the intentions and progress of your associations, I availed myself of the opportunity offered by your character and situation, to propose to you inquiries *as to facts*, which would make those *developments so important to be known by our people*. My inquiries were framed to draw out *full and authentic details* of the organization, numbers, resources, and designs of the abolitionists, of the means they resorted to for the accomplishment of their ends, and the progress made, and making, in their dangerous work, that all such information might be laid before the *four millions and a half of white inhabitants in the slave States, whose lives and property are menaced and endangered* by this ill-considered, misnamed, and disorganizing philanthropy. They should be informed of the full length and breadth and depth of this storm which is gathering over their heads, before it breaks in its desolating fury. Christians and civilized, they are *now* industrious, prosperous, and happy ; but should your schemes of abolition prevail, it will bring upon them overwhelming ruin, and misery unutterable. The two races cannot exist together upon terms of equality —the extirpation of one and the ruin of the other *would be inevitable.* This humanity, conceived in wrong and born in civil strife, would be baptized in a people's blood. It was, that our people might know, in time to guard against the mad onset, the full extent of this gigantic conspiracy and crusade against their institutions ; and of necessity upon their lives with which they must sustain them ; and their fortunes and prosperity, which *exist only while these institutions exist*, that I· was induced to enter into a correspondence with you, who by your official station and intelligence were known to be well informed on these points, and from your well established character for candor and fairness, would make no statements of facts which were not known or believed by you to be true. To a great extent, my end has been accomplished by your replies to my inquiries. How far, or whether at all, your answers have run, beyond *the facts inquired for*, into theories, argumer.ts, and dissertations, as erroneous as mischievous, is not a matter of present consideration. We differed no wider than I expected, but that difference has been exhibited courteously, and has nothing to do with the question of publication. Your object, or rather the object of your Committee, is to publish; and I, having no reason to desire it, as you have put me in possession of the facts I wished, and no reason not to desire it, as there is nothing to conceal, will leave yourself and the Committee to take your own course, neither assenting nor dissenting, in what you may finally decide to do.

Very respectfully,
Your obedient servant,
" F. H. Elmore."

[This letter of Mr. Elmore contains but little more than a reiteration of alarming cries on the part of the slaveholder ;—cries that are as old as the earliest attempts of philanthropy to break the fetters of the enslaved, and that have been repeated up to the present day, with a boldness that seems to increase, as instances of emancipation multiply to prove them groundless. Those who utter them seem, in their panic, not only to overlook the most obvious laws of the human mind, and the lights of experience, but to be almost unconscious of the great events connected with slavery, that are now passing around them in the world, and conspiring to bring about its early abrogation among all civilized and commercial nations.

However *Christian and civilized, industrious, prosperous and happy*, the SLAVHOLDERS of the South may be, this cannot be said of the SLAVES. A large religious denomination of the state in which Mr. Elmore resides, has deliberately pronounced them to be " HEATHEN." *Their* " industry" is seen at the end of the lash—of " prosperity" they have none, for they cannot possess any thing that is an element of prosperity —their " happiness" they prove, by running away from their masters, whenever they think they can effect their escape. This is the condition of a large *majority* of the people in South Carolina, Mississippi and Louisiana.

The " two races" exist in peace in Mexico,—in all the former South American dependencies of Spain, in Antigua, in the Bermudas, in Canada, in Massachusetts, in Vermont, in fine, in every country where they enjoy *legal equality*. It is the *denial* of this that produces discontent. MEN will never be satisfied without it. Let the slaveholders consult the irreversible laws of the human mind—make a full concession of right to those from whom they have withheld it, and they will be blessed with a peace, political, social, moral, beyond their present conceptions ; without such concessions they never can possess it.

A system that cannot withstand the assaults of truth—that replies to arguments with threats—that cannot be " talked about"—that flourishes in secrecy and darkness, and dies when brought forth into the light and examined, must in this time of inexorable scrutiny and relentless agitation, be a dangerous one. If *justice* be done, all necessity for the extirpation of any part of the people will at once be removed. Baptisms *of blood* are seen only when humanity has failed in her offices, and the suffering discern hope only in the brute efforts of despair.

Mr. Elmore is doubtless well versed in general history. To his vigorous declamation, I reply by asking, if he can produce from the history of our race a single instance, where emancipation, full and immediate, has been followed, as a legitimate consequence, by insurrection or bloodshed. I may go further, and ask him for a well authenticated instance, where an emancipated slave, singly has imbrued his hands in his master's blood. The first record of such an act in modern times, is yet to be made.

Mr. Elmore says " the white inhabitants in the slave states should be informed of the full length and breadth and depth of this storm which is gathering over their heads, before it breaks in its desolating fury." In this sentiment there is not a reasonable man in the country, be he abolitionist or not, who will not coincide with him. We rejoice at the evidence we here have, in a gentleman of the influence and intelligence of Mr. Elmore, of the returning sanity of the South. How wildly and mischievously has she been heretofore misled ! Whilst the Governors of Virginia, Alabama, Tennessee and Arkansas, have been repelling offers, made in respectful terms, of the fullest and most authentic accounts of our movements ; and whilst Governor Butler of South Carolina, has not only followed the example of his gubernatorial brethren just named, but is found corresponding with an obscure culprit in Massachusetts—bribing him with a few dollars, the sum he demanded for his fraudulent promise to aid in thwarting the abolitionists* ; whilst too, Mr. Calhoun has been willing to pass laws to shut out from his constituents and the South generally information that concerned them more nearly than all others—we now have it from the highest source, from one selected by a state delegation as its *representative* in a general committee of the whole slaveholding delegations, that the South ought to be " *informed of the full length and breadth*

* Appendix, H.

and depth" of the measures, intentions, &c, of the abolitionists. At this there is not an abolitionist who will not rejoice. We ask for nothing but access to the popular mind of the South. We feel full confidence in the eternal rectitude of our principles, and of their reception at the South, when once they are understood. Let the conflict come, let the truth of liberty fairly enter the lists with the error of slavery, and we have not a doubt of a glorious triumph.

May we not, after this, expect the aid of Mr. Elmore and others of equal distinction in the South, in giving to their fellow-citizens the information that we have always believed, and that they now acknowledge, to be so important to them?

May 24, 1838.   JAMES G. BIRNEY.]

APPENDIX.

APPENDIX A.

EXTRACT from an article addressed to the editor of the Christian Register and Observer, signed W. E. C.—attributed to the Rev. Dr. Channing.

"Speaking of slavery, I wish to recommend to your readers a book just from the press, entitled 'Emancipation in the West Indies,' and written by J. A. Thome and J. H. Kimball, who had visited those islands to inquire into the great experiment now going on there. I regard it as the most important work which has appeared among us for years. No man, without reading it, should undertake to pass judgment on Emancipation. It is something more than a report of the observation and opinions of the writers. It consists, chiefly, of the opinions, conversations, letters, and other documents of the very inhabitants of the islands whose judgments are most trust-worthy; of the governors, special magistrates, police officers, managers, attorneys, physicians, &c; and, in most cases, the names of these individuals are given, so that we have the strongest evidence of the correctness of the work.

"The results of this great experiment surpass what the most sanguine could have hoped. It is hardly possible that the trial could have been made under more unfavorable circumstances. The planters on all the islands were opposed to the Act of Emancipation, and, in most, exceedingly and fiercely hostile to it, and utterly indisposed to give it the best chance of success. The disproportion of the colored race to the whites was fearfully great, being that of seven or eight to one; whilst, in our slaveholding states, the whites outnumber the colored people. The slaves of the West Indies were less civilized than ours, and less fit to be trusted with their own support. Another great evil was, that the proprietors, to a considerable extent, were absentees; residing in England, and leaving the care of their estates and slaves to managers and owners; the last people for such a trust, and utterly unfit to carry the wretched victims of their tyranny through the solemn transition from slavery to freedom. To complete the unhappy circumstances under which the experiment began, the Act of Emancipation was passed by a distant government, having no intimate knowledge of the subject; and the consequence was, that a system of 'Apprenticeship,' as it was called, was adopted, so absurd, and betraying such ignorance of the principles of human nature, that, did we not know otherwise, we might suspect its author of intending to produce a failure. It was to witness the results of an experiment promising so little good, that our authors visited three islands, particularly worthy of examination—Antigua, Barbadoes, and Jamaica.

" Our authors went first to Antigua, an island which had been wise enough to foresee the mischiefs of the proposed apprenticeship, and had substituted for it immediate and unqualified emancipation. The report given of this island is most cheering. It is, indeed, one of the brightest records in history The account, beginning page 143, of the transition from slavery to freedom, can hardly be read by a man of ordinary sensibility without a thrill of tender and holy joy. Why is it not published in all our newspapers as among the most interesting events of our age? From the accounts of Antigua, it appears that immediate emancipation has produced only good. Its fruits are, greater security, the removal of the fears which accompany slavery, better and cheaper cultivation of the soil, increased value of real estate, improved morals, more fiequent marriages, and fewer crimes. *The people proclaim, with one voice, that emancipation is a blessing, and that nothing would tempt them to revert to slavery.*

" Our authors proceeded next to Barbadoes, where the apprenticeship system is in operation; and if any proof were needed of the docility and good dispositions of the negroes, it would be found in their acquiescence to so wonderful a degree in this unhappy arrangement. The planters on this island have been more disposed, than could have been anticipated, to make the best of this system, and here, accordingly, the same fruits of the Act of Emancipation are found as in Antigua, though less abundant; and a very general and strong conviction prevails of the happiness of the change.

" In Jamaica, apprenticeship manifests its worst tendencies. The planters of this island were, from first to last, furious in their hostility to the act of emancipation; and the effort seems to have been, to make the apprenticeship bear as heavily as possible on the colored people; so that, instead of preparing them for complete emancipation, it has rather unfitted them for this boon. Still, under all these disadvantages, there is strong reason for expecting, that emancipation, when it shall come, will prove a great good. At any rate, it is hardly possible for the slaves to fall into a more deplorable condition, than that in which this interposition of parliament found them.

" The degree of success which has attended this experiment in the West Indies, under such unfavorable auspices, makes us sure, that emancipation in this country, accorded by the good will of the masters, would be attended with the happiest effects. One thing is plain, that it would be perfectly *safe*. Never were the West Indies so peaceful and secure as since emancipation. So far from general massacre and insurrection, not an instance is recorded or intimated of violence of any kind being offered to a white man. Our authors were continually met by assurances of security on the part of the planters, so that, in this respect at least, emancipation has been unspeakable gain. The only obstacle to emancipation is, therefore, removed; for nothing but well grounded fears of violence and crime can authorize a man to encroach one moment on another's freedom.

" The subject of this book is of great interest at the present moment. Slavery, in the abstract, has been thoroughly discussed among us. We all agree that it is a great wrong. Not a voice is here lifted up in defence of the system, when viewed in a general light. We only differ when we come to apply our principles to a particular case. The only question is, whether the Southern states can abolish slavery consistently with the public safety, order, and peace? Many, very many well disposed people, both at the North and South, are possessed with vague fears of massacre and universal misrule, as the consequences of emancipation. Such ought to inquire into the ground of their alarm. They are bound to listen to the voice of *facts*, and such are given in this book. None of us have a right to make up our minds without inquiry, or to rest in opinions adopted indolently and without thought. It is a great crime to doom millions of our race to brutal degradation, on the ground of unreasonable fears. The power of public opinion is here irresistible, and to this power every man contributes something; so that every man, by his spirit and language, helps to loosen or rivet the chains of the slave."

The following sentiments are expressed by GOVERNOR EVERETT, of Massachusetts, in a letter to EDMUND QUINCY, Esq., dated

"BOSTON, *April* 29, 1838.

"DEAR SIR,—I have your favor of the 21st, accompanied with the volume containing the account of the tour of Messrs. Thome and Kimball in the West Indies, for which you will be pleased to accept my thanks. I have perused this highly interesting narrative with the greatest satisfaction. From the moment of the passage of the law, making provision for the immediate or prospective abolition of slavery in the British colonial possessions, I have looked with the deepest solicitude for tidings of its operation. The success of the measure, as it seemed to me, would afford a better hope than had before existed, that a like blessing might be enjoyed by those portions of the United States where slavery prevails. The only ground on which I had been accustomed to hear the continuance of slavery defended at the South, was that of necessity, and the impossibility of abolishing it without producing consequences of the most disastrous character to both parties. The passage of a law providing for the emancipation of nearly a million of slaves in the British colonies, seemed to afford full opportunity of bringing this momentous question to the decisive test of experience. *If the result proved satisfactory, I have never doubted that it would seal the fate of slavery throughout the civilized world.* As far as the observations of Messrs. Thome and Kimball extended, the result is of the most gratifying character. It appears to place beyond a doubt, that the experiment of immediate emancipation, adopted by the colonial Legislature of Antigua, has fully succeeded in that island; and the plan of apprenticeship in other portions of the West Indies, as well as could have been expected from the obvious inherent vices of that measure. *It has given me new views of the practicability of emancipation.* It has been effected in Antigua, as appears from unquestionable authorities contained in the work of Messrs. Thome and Kimball, not merely *without danger* to the master, but without any sacrifice of his *interest*. I cannot but think that the information collected in the volume will have a powerful effect on public opinion, not only in the northern states, but in the slaveholding states."

GOVERNOR ELLSWORTH, of Connecticut, writes thus to A. F. WILLIAMS, Esq., of this city :—

"NEW HAVEN, *May* 19, 1838.

"MY DEAR SIR,—Just before I left home, I received from you the Journal of Thome and Kimball, for which token of friendship I intended to have made you my acknowledgments before this; but I wished first to read the book. As far as time would permit, I have gone over most of its pages; and let me assure you, it is justly calculated to produce great effects, provided you can once get it into the hands of the planters. Convince *them* that their interests, as well as their security, will be advanced by employing free blacks, and emancipation will be accomplished without difficulty or delay.

"I have looked with great interest at the startling measure of emancipation in Antigua; but if this book is correct, the question is settled as to that island beyond a doubt, since there is such accumulated testimony from all classes, that the business and real estate of the island have advanced, by reason of the emancipation, one fourth, at least, in value; while personal security, without military force, is felt by the former masters, and contentment, industry, and gratitude, are seen in those who were slaves.

"The great moral example of England, in abolishing slavery in the West Indies, will produce a revolution on this subject throughout the world, and put down slavery in every Christian country.

"With sentiments of high esteem, &c,

"W. W. ELLSWORTH."

APPENDIX B.

A short time previous to the late election in Rhode Island for governor and lieutenant-governor, a letter was addressed to each of the candidates for those offices by Mr. Johnson, Corresponding Secretary of the Rhode Island Anti-Slavery Society, embodying the views of the abolitionists on the several subjects it embraced, in a series of queries. Their purport will appear from the answer of Mr. Sprague, (who was elected governor,) given below. The answer of Mr. Childs (elected lieutenant-governor) is fully as direct as that of governor Sprague.

"WARWICK, *March* 28, 1838.

"DEAR SIR,—Your favor of the 19th inst. requesting of me, in conformity to a resolution of the Executive Committee of the Rhode Island Anti-Slavery Society, an expression of my opinions on certain topics, was duly received. I have no motive whatever for withholding my opinions on any subject which is interesting to any portion of my fellow-citizens. I will, therefore, cheerfully proceed to reply to the interrogatories proposed, and in the order in which they are submitted.

"1. Among the powers vested by the Constitution in Congress, is the power to exercise exclusive legislation, 'in all cases whatsoever,' over the District of Columbia? 'All cases' must, of course, include the *case* of slavery and the slave-trade. I am, therefore, clearly of opinion, that the Constitution does confer upon Congress the power to abolish slavery and the slave-trade in that District; and, as they are great moral and political evils, the principles of justice and humanity demand the exercise of that power.

"2. The traffic in slaves, whether foreign or domestic, is equally obnoxious to every principle of justice and humanity; and, as Congress has exercised its powers to suppress the slave-trade between this country and foreign nations, it ought, as a matter of consistency and justice, to exercise the same powers to suppress the slave-trade between the states of this Union. The slave-trade within the states is, undoubtedly, beyond the control of Congress; as the 'sovereignty of each state, to legislate exclusively on the subject of slavery, which is tolerated within its limits,' is, I believe, universally conceded. The Constitution unquestionably recognises the sovereign power of each state to legislate on the subject within its limits; but it imposes on us no obligation to add to the evils of the system by countenancing the traffic between the states. That which our laws have solemnly pronounced to be piracy in our oreign intercourse, no sophistry can make honorable or justifiable in a domestic form. For a proof of the feelings which this traffic naturally inspires, we need but refer to the universal execration in which the slave-dealer is held in those portions of the country where the institution of slavery is guarded with the most jealous vigilance.

" 3. Congress has no power to abridge the right of petition. The right of the people of the non-slaveholding states to petition Congress for the abolition of slavery and the slave-trade in the District of Columbia, and the traffic of human beings among the states, is as undoubted as any right guarantied by the Constitution ; and I regard the Resolution which was adopted by the House of Representatives on the 21st of December last as a virtual denial of that right, inasmuch as it disposed of all such petitions, as might be presented thereafter, in advance of presentation and reception. If it was right thus to dispose of petitions on *one* subject, it would be equally right to dispose of them in the same manner on *all* subjects, and thus cut of all communication, by petition, between the people and their representatives. Nothing can be more clearly a violation of the spirit of the Constitution, as it rendered utterly nugatory a right which was considered of such vast importance as to be specially guarantied in that sacred instrument. A similar Resolution passed the House of Representatives at the first session of the last Congress, and as I then entertained the same views which I have now expressed, I recorded my vote against it.

" 4. I fully concur in the sentiment, that ' every principle of justice and humanity requires, that every human being, when personal freedom is at stake, should have the benefit of a jury trial ;' and I have no hesitation in saying, that the laws of this state ought to secure that benefit, so far as they can, to persons claimed as fugitives from ' service or labor,' without interfering with the laws of the United States. The course pursued in relation to this subject by the Legislature of Massachusetts meets my approbation.

" 5. I am opposed to all attempts to abridge or restrain the freedom of speech and the press, or to forbid any portion of the people peaceably to assemble to discuss any subject—moral, political, or religious.

" 6. I am opposed to the annexation of Texas to the United States

" 7. It is undoubtedly inconsistent with the principles of a free state, professing to be governed in its legislation by the principles of freedom, to sanction slavery, in any form, within its jurisdiction. If we have laws in this state which bear this construction, they ought to be repealed. We should extend to our southern brethren, whenever they may have occasion to come among us, all the privileges and immunities enjoyed by our own citizens, and all the rights and privileges guarantied to them by the Constitution of the United States ; but they cannot expect of us to depart from the fundamental principles of civil liberty for the purpose of obviating any temporal inconvenience which they may experience.

" These are my views upon the topics proposed for my consideration. They are the views which I have always entertained, (at least ever since I have been awakened to their vast importance,) and which I have always supported, so far as I could, by my vote in Congress ; and if, in any respect, my answers have not been sufficiently explicit, it will afford me pleasure to reply to any other questions which you may think proper to propose.

" I am, Sir, very respectfully,
" Your friend and fellow citizen,
" WILLIAM SPRAGUE."

OLIVER JOHNSON, Esq., Cor. Sec. R. I. A. S. Society.

APPENDIX C.

The abolitionists in Connecticut petitioned the Legislature of that state at its late session on several subjects deemed by them proper for legislative action. In answer to these petitions—

1. The law known as the "Black Act" or the "Canterbury law"—under which Miss Crandall was indicted and tried—was repealed, except a single provision, which is not considered objectionable.

2. The right to *trial by jury* was secured to persons who are claimed as slaves.

3. Resolutions were passed asserting the power of Congress to abolish slavery in the District of Columbia, and recommending that it be done as soon as it can be, "consistently with the *best good* of the *whole* country." (!)

4. Resolutions were passed protesting against the annexation of Texas to the Union.

5. Resolutions were passed asserting the right of petition as inalienable—condemning Mr. Patton's resolution of Dec. 21, 1837 as an invasion of the rights of the people, and calling on the Connecticut delegation in Congress to use their efforts to have the same rescinded.

APPENDIX D.

In the year 1793 there were but 5,000,000 pounds of cotton produced in the United States, and but 500,000 exported. Cotton never could have become an article of much commercial importance under the old method of preparing it for market. By hand-picking, or by a process strictly *manual*, a cultivator could not prepare for market, during the year, more than from 200 to 300 pounds; being only about one-tenth of what he could cultivate to maturity in the field. In '93 Mr. Whitney invented the Cotton-gin now in use, by which the labor of at least *one thousand* hands under the old system, is performed by *one*, in preparing the crop for market. Seven years after the invention (1800) 35,000,000 pounds were raised, and 17,800,000 exported. In 1834, 460,000,000 were raised—384,750,000 exported. Such was the effect of Mr. Whitney's invention. It gave, at once, extraordinary value to the *land* in that part of the country where alone cotton could be raised; and to *slaves*, because it was the general, the almost universal, impression that the cultivation of the South could be carried on only by slaves. There being no *free* state in the South, competition between free and slave labor never could exist on a scale sufficiently extensive to prove the superiority of the former in the production of cotton, and in the preparation of it for market.

Thus, it has happened that Mr. Whitney has been the innocent occasion of giving to slavery in this country its present importance—of magnifying it into the great interest to which all others must yield. How he was rewarded by the South—especially by the planters of Georgia—the reader may see by consulting Silliman's Journal for January, 1832, and the Encyclopædia Americana, article, WHITNEY.

APPENDIX E.

It is impossible, of course, to pronounce with precision, how great would have been the effect in favor of emancipation, if the effort to resist the admission of Missouri as a slaveholding state had been successful. We can only conjecture what it would have been, by the effect its admission has had in fostering slavery up to its present huge growth and pretensions. If the American people had shown, through their National legislature, a *sincere* opposition to slavery by the rejection of Missouri, it is probable at least—late as it was—that the early expiration of the 'system' would, by this time, have been discerned by all men.

When the Constitution was formed, the state of public sentiment even in the South—with the exception of South Carolina and Georgia, was favorable to emancipation. Under the influence of this public sentiment was the Constitution formed. No person at all versed in constitutional or legal interpretation—with his judgment unaffected by interest or any of the prejudices to which the existing controversy has given birth—could, it is thought, construe the Constitution, *in its letter*, as intending to perpetuate slavery. To come to such a conclusion with a full knowledge of what was the mind of this nation in regard to slavery, when that instrument was made, demonstrates a moral or intellectual flaw that makes all reasoning useless.

Although it is a fact beyond controversy in our history, that the power conferred by the Constitution on Congress to "regulate commerce with foreign nations" was known to include the power of abolishing the African slave-trade—and that it was expected that Congress, at the end of the period for which the exercise of that power on this particular subject was restrained, would use it (as it did) *with a view to the influence that the cutting off of that traffic would have on the "system" in this country*—yet, such has been the influence of the action of Congress on all matters with which slavery has been mingled—more especially on the Missouri question, in which slavery was the sole interest—that an impression has been produced on the popular mind, that the Constitution of the United States *guaranties*, and consequently *perpetuates*, slavery to the South. Most artfully, incessantly, and powerfully, has this lamentable error been harped on by the slaveholders, and by their advocates in the free states. The impression of *constitutional favor* to the slaveholders would, of itself, naturally create for them an undue and disproportionate influence in the control of the government ; but when to this is added the arrogance that the possession of irresponsible power almost invariably engenders in its possessors—their overreaching assumptions—the contempt that the slaveholders entertain for the great body of the *people* of the North, it has almost delivered over the government, bound neck and heels, into the hands of slaveholding politicians—to be bound still more rigorously, or unloosed, as may seem well in their discretion.

Who can doubt that, as a nation, we should have been more honorable and influen tial abroad—more prosperous and united at home—if Kentucky, at the very outset of this matter, had been refused admission to the Union until she had expunged from her Constitution the covenant with oppression ? She would not have remained out of the Union a single year on that account. If the worship of Liberty had not been exchanged for that of Power—if her principles had been successfully maintained in this first assault, their triumph in every other would have been easy. We should not have had a state less in the confederacy, and slavery would have been seen, at this time, shrunk up to the most contemptible dimensions, if it had not vanished entirely away. But we have furnished another instance to be added to the long and melancholy list already existing, to prove that,—

————————"facilis descensus Averni,
Sed revocare gradum ——————————
Hoc opus hic labor est,"——————————

if *poetry* is not *fiction*.

Success in the Missouri struggle—late as it was—would have placed the cause of freedom in our country out of the reach of danger from its inexorable foe. The principles of liberty would have struck deeper root in the free states, and have derived fresh vigor from such a triumph. If these principles had been honored by the government from that period to the present, (as they would have been, had the free states, even then, assumed their just preponderance in its administration,) we should now have, in Missouri herself, a healthful and vigorous ally in the cause of freedom; and, in Arkansas, a free people—*twice* her present numbers—pressing on the confines of slavery, and summoning the keepers of the southern charnel-house to open its doors, that its inmates might walk forth, in a glorious resurrection to liberty and life. Although young, as a people, we should be, among the nations, venerable for our virtue; and we should exercise an influence on the civilized and commercial world that we must despair of possessing, as long as we remain vulnerable to every shaft that malice, or satire, or philanthropy may find it convenient to hurl against us.*

Instead of being thus seated on a "heaven-kissing hill," and seen of all in its pure radiance; instead of enjoying its delightful airs, and imparting to them the healthful savor of justice, truth, mercy, magnanimity, see what a picture we present;—our cannibal burnings of human beings—our Lynch courts—our lawless scourgings and capital executions, not only of slaves, but of freemen—our demoniac mobs raging through the streets of our cities and large towns at midday as well as at midnight, shedding innocent blood, devastating property, and applying the incendiaries' torch to edifices erected and dedicated to FREE DISCUSSION—the known friends of order, of law, of liberty, of the Constitution—citizens, distinguished for their worth at home, and reflecting honor on their country abroad, shut out from more than half our territory, or visiting it at the hazard of their lives, or of the most degrading and painful personal inflictions—freedom of speech and of the press overthrown and hooted at—the right of petition struck down in Congress, where, above all places, it ought to have been maintained to the last—the people mocked at, and attempted to be gagged by their own servants—the time the office-honored veteran, who fearlessly contended for the *right*, publicly menaced for words spoken in his place as a representative of the people, with an indictment by a slaveholding grand jury—in fine, the great principles of government asserted by our fathers in the Declaration of Independence, and embodied in our Constitution, with which they won for us the sympathy, the admiration of the world—all forgotten, dishonoured, despised, trodden under foot! And this for slavery!!

Horrible catalogue!—yet by no means a complete one—for so young a nation; boasting itself, too, to be the freest on earth! It is the ripe fruit of that *chef d'œuvre* of political skill and patriotic achievement—the MISSOURI COMPROMISE.

Another such compromise—or *any* compromise now with slavery—and the nation is undone.

---

* A comic piece—the production of one of the most popular of the French writers in his way—had possession of the Paris stage last winter. When one of the personages SEPARATES HUSBAND AND WIFE, he cries out, "BRAVO! THIS IS THE DECLARATION OF INDEPENDENCE OF THE UNITED STATES!" [Bravo! C'est la Declaration d'Independence des Etats Unis.]

One of our distinguished College-professors, lately on a tour in Europe, had his attention called, while passing along the street of a German city, to the pictorial representation of a WHITE MAN SCOURGING A SUPPLICATING COLORED FEMALE, with this allusion underwritten:—"A SPECIMEN OF EQUALITY—FROM REPUBLICAN AMERICA."

Truly might our countryman have exclaimed in the language, if not with the generous emotions of the Trojan hero, when he beheld the noble deeds of his countrymen pencilled in a strange land—

_____ " Quis jam locus—
Quæ regio in terris nostri non plena laboris?"

APPENDIX F.

The following is believed to be a correct exhibit of the legislative resolutions against the annexation of Texas—of the *times* at which they were passed, and of the *votes* by which they were passed :—

1. VERMONT.

" 1. *Resolved, By the Senate and House of Representatives*, That our Senators in Congress be instructed, and our Representatives requested, to use their influence in that body to prevent the annexation of Texas to the Union.

" 2. *Resolved*, That representing, as we do, the people of Vermont, we do hereby, in their name, SOLEMNLY PROTEST against such annexation in any form."

[Passed unanimously, Nov. 1, 1837.]

2. RHODE ISLAND.

(*In General Assembly, October Session, A. D.* 1837.)

" Whereas the compact of the Union between these states was entered into by the people thereof in their respective states, ' in order to form a more perfect Union, establish justice, ensure domestic tranquillity, provide for the common defence, promote the general welfare, and secure the blessings of liberty to themselves and their posterity ;' and, therefore, a Representative Government was instituted by them, with certain limited powers, clearly specified and defined in the Constitution—all other powers, not therein expressly relinquished, being ' reserved to the states respectively, or to the people.'

" And whereas this limited government possesses no power to extend its jurisdiction over any foreign nation, and no foreign nation, country, or people, can be admitted into this Union but by the sovereign will and act of the free people of all and each of these United States, nor without the formation of a new compact of Union—and another frame of government radically different, in objects, principles, and powers, from that which was framed for our own self-government, and deemed to be adequate to all the exigencies of our own free republic :—

" Therefore, Resolved, That we have witnessed, with deep concern, the indications of a disposition to bring into this Union, as a constituent member thereof, the foreign province or territory of Texas.

" Resolved, That, although we are fully aware of the consequences which must follow the accomplishment of such a project, could it be accomplished—aware that it would lead speedily to the conquest and annexation of Mexico itself, and its fourteen remaining provinces or intendencies—which, together with the revolted province of Texas, would furnish foreign territories and foreign people for at least twenty members of the new Union ; that the government of a nation so extended and so constructed would soon become radically [changed] in character, if not in form—would unavoidably become a military government ; and, under the plea of necessity, would free itself from the restraints of the Constitution and from its accountability to the people. That the ties of kindred, common origin and common interests, which have so long bound this people together, and would still continue to bind them ; these ties, which ought to be held sacred by all true Americans, would be angrily dissolved, and sectional political combinations would be formed with the newly admitted foreign states, unnatural and adverse to the peace and prosperity of the country. The civil government, with all the arbitrary powers it might assume, would be unable to control the storm. The usurper would find himself in his proper element; and, after acting the patriot and the hero for a due season, as the only means of rescuing the country from the ruin which he had chiefly contributed to bring upon it, would reluctantly and modestly allow himself to be declared ' Protector of the Commonwealth.'

" We are now fully aware of the deep degradation into which the republic would sink itself in the eyes of the whole world, should it annex to its own vast territories other and foreign territories of immense though unknown extent, for the purpose of encouraging the propagation of slavery, and giving aid to the raising of slaves within its own bosom, the very bosom of freedom, to be exported and sold in those unhallowed regions. Although we are fully aware of these fearful evils, and numberless others which would come in their train, yet we do not here dwell upon them; because we are here firmly convinced that the free people of most, and we trust of all these states, will never suffer the admission of the foreign territory of Texas into this Union as a constituent member thereof—will never suffer the integrity of this Republic to be violated, either by the introduction and addition to it of foreign nations or territories, one or many, or by dismemberment of it by the transfer of any one or more of its members to a foreign nation. The people will be aware, that should one foreign state or country be introduced, another and another may be, without end, whether situated in South America, in the West India islands, or in any other part of the world; and that a single foreign state, thus admitted, might have in its power, by holding the balance between contending parties, to wrest their own government from the hands and control of the people, by whom it was established for their own benefit and self-government. We are firmly convinced, that the free people of these states will look upon any attempt to introduce the foreign territory of Texas, or any other foreign territory or nation into this Union, as a constituent member or members thereof, as manifesting a willingness to prostrate the Constitution and dissolve the Union.

" Resolved, That His Excellency, the Governor, be requested to forward a copy of the foregoing resolutions to each of our Senators and Representatives in Congress, and to each of the Executives of the several states, with a request that the same may be laid before the respective Legislatures of said states."

[The Preamble and Resolutions were unanimously adopted, Nov. 3, 1837.]

3. OHIO.

" *Resolved, by the General Assembly of the State of Ohio*, That in the name, and on behalf of the people of the State of Ohio, we do hereby SOLEMNLY PROTEST against the annexation of Texas to the Union of these United States.

" *And be it further resolved*, That the Governor be requested to transmit to each of our Senators and Representatives in Congress, and to the Governors of each of the States, a copy of the foregoing resolution, with a statement of the votes by which it was passed in each branch of the Legislature.

[Passed by 64 out of 72, the whole number in the House of Representatives—unanimously in the Senate. Feb. 24, 1838.]

4. MASSACHUSETTS.

" Resolves against the annexation of Texas to the United States.

" Whereas a proposition to admit into the United States as a constituent member thereof, the foreign nation of Texas, has been recommended by the legislative resolutions of several States, and brought before Congress for its approval and sanction ; and whereas such a measure would involve great wrong to Mexico, and otherwise be of evil precedent, injurious to the interests and dishonorable to the character of this country ; and whereas its avowed óbjects are doubly fraught with peril to the prosperity and permanence of this Union, as tending to disturb and destroy the conditions of those compromises and concessions, entered into at the formation of the Constitution, by which the relative weights of different sections and interests were adjusted, and to strengthen and extend the evils of a system which is unjust in itself, in striking contrast with the theory of our institutions, and condemned by the moral sentiment of mankind ; and whereas the people of these United States have not granted to any or all of the departments of their Government, but have retained in themselves, the only power adequate to the admission of a foreign nation into this confederacy ; therefore,

" *Resolved*, That we, the Senate and House of Representatives, in General Court assembled, do in the name of the people of Massachusetts, earnestly and solemnly protest against the incorporation of Texas into this Union, and declare, that no act done or compact made, for such purpose by the government of the United States, will be binding on the States or the People.

" *Resolved*, That his Excellency the Governor be requested to forward a copy of these resolutions and the accompanying report to the Executive of the United States, and the Executive of each State and also to each of our Senators and Representatives in Congress, with a request that they present the resolves to both Houses of Congress."

[Passed MARCH 16, 1838, UNANIMOUSLY, in both Houses.]

5. MICHIGAN.

Whereas, propositions have been made for the annexation of Texas to the United States, with a view to its ultimate incorporation into the Union :

" And whereas, the extension of this General Government over so large a country on the south-west, between which and that of the original states, there is little affinity, and less identity of interest, would tend, in the opinion of this Legislature, greatly to disturb the safe and harmonious operations of the Government of the United States, and put in imminent danger the continuance of this happy Union : Therefore,

" *Be it resolved, by the Senate and House of Representatives of the State of Michigan*, That in behalf, and in the name of the State of Michigan, this Legislature doth hereby dissent from, and solemnly protest against the annexation, for any purpose, to this Union, of Texas, or of any oiher territory or district of country, heretofore constituting a part of the dominions of Spain in America, lying west or south-west of Louisiana."

" And be it further Resolved, by the Authority aforesaid, That the Governor of this State be requested to transmit a copy of the foregoing preamble and resolve, under the great seal of this state, to the President of the United States ; also, that he transmit one copy thereof, authenticated in manner aforesaid, to the President of the Senate of the United States, with the respectful request of this Legislature, that the same may be laid before the Senate ; also, that he transmit one copy thereof to the Speaker of the House of Representatives of the United States, authenticated in like manner, with the respectful request of this Legislature, that the same may be laid before the House of Representatives; and also, that he transmit to each of our Senators and Representatives in Congress, one copy thereof, together with the Report adopted by this Legislature, and which accompanies said preamble and resolves.

[Passed nearly if not quite unanimously, April 2, 1838].

---

6. CONNECTICUT.

"*Resolved*, That we, the Senate and House of Representatives in General Assembly convened, do, in the name of the people of this State, solemnly *protest* against the annexation of Texas to this Union.

[Passed, it is believed, unanimously in both houses.]

[Those which follow were passed by but one branch of the respective Legislatures in which they were introduced.]

7. PENNSYLVANIA.

Resolutions relative to the admission of Texas into the Union.

"*Whereas* the annexation of Texas to the United States has been advocated and strongly urged by many of our fellow-citizens, particularly in the southern part of our country, and the president of Texas has received authority to open a correspondence with, and appoint, a commissioner to our government to accomplish the object ;—*And whereas* such a measure would bring to us a dangerous extension of territory, with a population generally not desirable, and would probably involve us in war ;—*And whereas* the subject is now pressed upon and agitated in Congress ; therefore,

"*Resolved*, &c, That our Senators in Congress be instructed, and our Representatives requested, to use their influence and vote against the annexation of Texas to the territory of the United States.

"*Resolved*, That the Governor transmit to each of our Senators and Representatives a copy of the foregoing preamble and resolutions."

[Passed the Senate March 9, 1838, by 22 to 6. Postponed indefinitely in the House of Representatives, April 13, by 41 to 39.]

---

8. MAINE.

"*Resolved*, That the Legislature of the State of Maine, on behalf of the people of said state, do earnestly and solemnly protest against the annexation of the Republic of Texas to these United States ; and that our Senators and Representatives in Congress be, and they hereby are, requested to exert their utmost influence to prevent the adoption of a measure at once so clearly unconstitutional, and so directly calculated to disturb our foreign relations, to destroy our domestic peace, and to dismember our blessed Union."

[Passed in the House of Representatives, March 22, 1838, by 85 to 30. Senate (same day) refused to concur by 11 to 10.]

---

9. NEW-YORK.

"*Resolved*, (if the Senate concur,) That the admission of the Republic of Texas into this Union would be entirely repugnant to the will of the people of this state, and would endanger the union of these United States.

"*Resolved*, (if the Senate concur,) That this Legislature do, in the name of the people of the State of New York, solemnly protest against the admission of the Republic of Texas into this Union.

" *Resolved*, (if the Senate concur,) That his Excellency the Governor be requested to transmit a copy of the foregoing resolutions to each of our Senators and Representatives in Congress, and also to the governors of each of the United States, with a request that the same be laid before their respective Legislatures."

[These resolutions passed the House of Representatives in April, by a large majority—the newspapers say, 83 to 13. They were indefinitely postponed in the Senate, by a vote of 21 to 9.]

APPENDIX G.

The number of petitioners for abolition in the District of Columbia, and on other subjects allied to it, have been ascertained (in the House of Representatives) to be as follows :—

	Men.	Women.	Total.
For abolition in the District,	51,366	78,882	130,248
Against the annexation of Texas,	104,973	77,419	182,392
Rescinding the gag resolution,	21,015	10,821	31,836
Against admitting any new slave state,	11,770	10,391	22,161
For abolition of the slave-trade between the states,	11,864	11,541	23,405
For abolition of slavery in tne territories,	9,129	12,083	21,212
At the extra session for rescinding the gag resolution of Jan. 21, 1837,	3,377		3,377
Total,	213,494	201,137	414,631

The number in the Senate, where some difficulty was interposed that prevented its being taken, is estimated to have been about two-thirds as great as that in the House.

APPENDIX H.

[On the 1st of December, one of the secretaries of the American Anti-Slavery Society addressed a note to each of the Governors of the slave states, in which he informed them, in courteous and respectful terms, that he had directed the Publishing Agent of this society, thereafter regularly to transmit to them, free of charge, the periodical publications issued from the office of the society. To this offer the following replies were received :—]

GOVERNOR CAMPBELL'S LETTER.

JAMES G. BIRNEY, Esq., *New York.*

" RICHMOND, *Dec.* 4, 1837.

" SIR,—I received, by yesterday's mail, your letter of the 1st instant, in which you state that you had directed the publishing agent of the American Anti-Slavery Society, hereafter, regularly to transmit, free of charge, by mail, to all the governors of the slave states, the periodical publications issued from that office.

" Regarding your society as highly mischievous, I decline receiving any communications from it, and must request that no publications from your office be transmitted to me.

" I am, &c,

" DAVID CAMPBELL."

GOVERNOR BAGBY'S LETTER.

" TUSCALOOSA, *Jan.* 6, 1838

" SIR,—I received, by due course of mail, your favor of the 1st of December, informing me that you had directed the publishing agent of the American Anti-Slavery Society to forward to the governors of the slaveholding states the periodicals issued from that office. Taking it for granted, that the only object which the society or yourself could have in view, in adopting this course, is, the dissemination of the opinions and principles of the society—having made up my own opinion, unalterably, in relation to the whole question of slavery, as it exists in a portion of the United States, and feeling confident that, in the correctness of this opinion, I am sustained by the entire free white population of Alabama, as well as the great body of the people of this Union, I must, with the greatest respect for yourself, personally—but not for the opinions or principles advocated by the society—positively decline receiving said publications, or any others of a similar character, either personally or officially. Indeed, it is presuming a little too much, to expect that the chief magistrate of a free people, elected by themselves, would hold correspondence or give currency to the publications of an organized society, openly engaged in a scheme fraught with more mischievous consequences to their interest and repose, than any that the wit or folly of mankind has heretofore devised.

" I am, very respectfully,

" Your ob't servant,

" A. P. BAGBY "

JAMES G. BIRNEY, Esq., *New York.*

GOVERNOR CANNON'S LETTER.

[This letter required so many alterations to bring it up to the ordinary standard of epistolary, grammatical, and orthographical accuracy, that it is thought best to give it, in *word* and *letter*, precisely as it was received at the office.]

" EXECUTIVE DEPT.——

" NASHVILLE, *Dec. 12th*, 1837.

" Sir

" I have rec'd yours of the 1st Inst notifying me, that you had directed, your periodical publications, on the subject of Slavery to be sent to me free of charge &c—and you are correct, if sincere, in your views, in supposing that we widely differ, on this subject, we do indeed widely differ, on it, if the publications said to have emanated from you, are honest and sincere, which, I admit, is possible.

" My opinions are fix'd and setled, and I seldom Look into or examine, the different vague notions of others who write and theorise on that subject, Hence I trust you will not expect me to examine, what you have printed on this subject, or cause to have printed, If you or any other man are influenced by feelings of humanity, and are laboring to relieve the sufferings, of the human race, you may find objects enough immediately around you, where you are, in any nonslaveholding State, to engage your, attention, and all your exertions, in that good cause.

" But if your aim is to make a flourish on the subject, before the world, and to gain yourself some notoriety, or distinction, without, doing good to any, and evil to many, of the human race, you are, pursuing the course calculated to effect, Such an object, in which no honest man need envy. Your honours, thus gaind, I know there are many such in our country, but would fain hope, you are not one of them, If you have Livd, as you state forty years in a Slave holding State, you know that, that class of its population, are not the most, miserable, degraded, or unhappy, either in their feelings or habits, You know they are generally governd, and provided for by men of information and understanding sufficient to guard them against the most, odious vices, and hibets of the country, from which, you know the slaves are in a far greater degree, exempt than, are other portions of the population. That the slaves are the most happy, moral and contented generally, and free from suffering of any kind, having each full confidence, in his masters, skill means and disposition to provide well for him, knowing also at the same time that *it is his interest to do it*, Hence in this State of Society more than any other, Superior intelligence has the ascendency, in governing and provideing, for the wants of those inferior, also in giveing direction to their Labour, and industry, as should be the case, superior intelligence Should govern, when united with Virtue, and interest, that great predominating principle in all human affairs It is my rule of Life, when I see any man labouring to produce effects, at a distance from him, while neglecting the objects immediately around him, (in doing good) to suspect his sincerity, to suspect him for some selfish, or sinister motive, all is not gold that glitters, and every man is not what he, endeavours to appear to be, is too well known It is the duty of masters to take care of there slaves and provide for them, and this duty I believe is as generally and as fully complyd with as any other duty enjoind on the human family, for next to their children their own offspring, their slaves stand next foremost in their care and attention, there are indeed very few instances of a contrary character.

"You can find around you, I doubt not a large number of persons intermix'd, in your society, who are entirely destitute of that care, and attention, towards them. that is enjoyed by our slaves, and who are destitute of that deep feeling of interest, in guarding their morals and habits, and directing them through Life in all things, which is here enjoyd by our slaves, to those let your efforts be directed immediately around you, and do not trouble with your vague speculations those who are contented and happy, at a distance from you.

"Very respectfully yours,

Mr. Jas. G. Birney, *Cor. Sec.* &c.   "N. Cannon."

[The letter of the Secretary to the governor of South Carolina was not *answered*, but was so inverted and folded as to present the *subscribed* name of the secretary, as the *superscription* of the same letter to be returned. The addition of *New York* to the address brought it back to this office.

Whilst governor Butler was thus refusing the information that was proffered to him in the most respectful terms from this office, he was engaged in another affair, having connection with the anti-slavery movement, as indiscreet, as it was unbecoming the dignity of the office he holds. The following account of it is from one of the Boston papers :—]

"*Hoaxing a Governor.*—The National Ægis says, that Hollis Parker, who was sentenced to the state prison at the late term of the criminal court for Worcester county, for endeavoring to extort money from governor Everett, had opened an extensive correspondence, previous to his arrest, with similar intent, with other distinguished men of the country. Besides several individuals in New York, governor Butler, of South Carolina, was honored with his notice. A letter from that gentleman, directed to Parker, was lately received at the post office in a town near Worcester, enclosing a check for fifty dollars. So far as the character of Parker's letter can be inferred from the reply of governor Butler, it would appear, that Parker informed the governor, that the design was entertained by some of our citizens, of transmitting to South Carolina a quantity of 'incendiary publications,' and that, with the aid of a little money, he (Parker) would be able to unravel the plot, and furnish full information concerning it to his excellency. The bait took, and the money was forwarded, with earnest appeals to Parker to be vigilant and active in thoroughly investigating the supposed conspiracy against the peace and happiness of the South.

"The Ægis has the following very just remarks touching this case :—'Governor Butler belongs to a state loud in its professions of regard for state rights and state sovereignty. We, also, are sincere advocates of that good old republican doctrine. It strikes us, that it would have comported better with the spirit of that doctrine, the dignity of his own station and character, the respect and courtesy due to a sovereign and independent state, if governor Butler had made the proper representation, if the subject was deserving of such notice, to the acknowledged head and-constituted authorities of that state, instead of holding official correspondence with a citizen of a foreign jurisdiction, and employing a secret agent and informer, whose very offer of such service was proof of the base and irresponsible character of him who made it.'"

GOVERNOR CONWAY'S LETTER.

"EXECUTIVE DEPARTMENT, LITTLE ROCK, ARKANSAS, *March* 1, 1838.

"SIR,—A newspaper, headed ' *The Emancipator*,' in which you are announced the 'publishing agent,' has, for some weeks past, arrived at the post office in this city, to my address. Not having subscribed, or authorized any individual to give my name as a subscriber, for that or any such paper, it is entirely *gratuitous* on the part of its publishers to send me a copy ; and not having a favorable opinion of the *intentions* of the *authors and founders* of the ' *American Anti-Slavery Society*,' I have to request a discontinuance of ' *The Emancipator*.'

"Your ob't servant,

"J. S. CONWAY."

R. G. WILLIAMS, Esq., *New York*.

[NOTE.—The following extract of a letter, from the late Chief Justice Jay to the late venerable Elias Boudinot, dated Nov. 17, 1819, might well have formed part of Appendix E. Its existence, however, was not known till it was too late to insert it in its most appropriate place. It will show the view taken of one of the *constitutional* questions by one of the most distinguished jurists, and one of the purest patriots, by whom our early history was illustrated.]

"Little can be added to what has been said and written on the subject of slavery. I concur in the opinion, that it ought not to be *introduced, nor permitted* in any of the *new* states ; and that it ought to be gradually diminished, and finally, abolished, in all of them.

"To me, the *constitutional authority* of the Congress to prohibit the *migration* and *importation* of slaves into any of the states, does not appear questionable.

"The first article of the Constitution specifies the legislative powers committed to Congress. The ninth section of that article has these words :—'The *migration* or *importation* of such persons as any of the *now existing* states shall think proper to admit, shall not be prohibited by the Congress prior to the year 1808—but a tax or duty may be imposed on such importation not exceeding *ten dollars* for each person.'

"I understand the sense and meaning of this clause to be, That the power of the Congress, although *competent to prohibit such migration and importation*, was not to be exercised with respect to the THEN existing states, and *them only*, until the year 1808 ; but that Congress were at liberty to make such prohibition as to any *new state* which might in the meantime be established. And further, that from and after *that* period, they were authorized to make such prohibition as to *all the states, whether new or old.*

"Slaves were the persons intended. The word slaves was avoided, on account of the existing toleration of slavery, and its discordancy with the principles of the Revolution ; and from a consciousness of its being repugnant to those propositions in the Declaration of Independence :—' We hold these truths to be self-evident—that all men are created equal—that they are endowed by their Creator with certain inalienable rights—and that, among these, are life, liberty, and the pursuit of happiness.'"